Zairema's Approach to the Bible

Zairema's Approach to the Bible

A Theological Appraisal

H. Laldintluanga

Christian World Imprints

First Published in 2020 by

Christian World Imprints
Christian Publishing & Books from India
C-3, Wazirpur Industrial Area
Delhi-110052
cwidelhi2017@gmail.com
www.ChristianWorldImprints.com
Phone: +91 11 41526079

ISBN: 978-93-5148-494-3 (HB)
ISBN: 978-93-5148-495-0 (PB)

Printed in India.

Contents

The book in its original form is the thesis submitted to the Senate of Serampore College (University) towards Master of Theology (M.Th.) degree and published it with permission from the Senate. The candidate is responsible for the contents, ideas and opinions expressed in the book. The title of the book is reframed to the present form for the purpose of publication.

Abstract

This thesis seeks to analyse the main thrust of Zairema's approach to the Bible and his contribution for providing a theoretical framework for social and moral reformation among the Mizo. The Biblicist section of the Mizo populace cannot understand Zairema's interpretation and ideology of translation of the Bible. They seldom understand that Jesus' Salvation is horizontal including socio-eco-political and religion (holistic salvation of humankind) but their understanding is limited only to a vertical ideology like, longing for departure from this miserable earthly life and to live in the place of all pleasures called heaven.

Since this study is an attempt to identify which aspects of Zairema's theology of the Bible are significant for the Mizo Christian and which are not, theological and contextual-liberative method is employed in this study. In order to facilitate this, Zairema's writings, which portray his theology and interpretation of the Bible, are studied. Apart from all available literatures relating to the subject, empirical study in the form of personal interviews with some selected figures was held according to necessity.

Like other Christian theologies, it is a human construction in a particular historical context. Its nature, characteristics and functions all are conditioned by its own context. All of the historical contexts played an important role in shaping Zairema's theology. It is fair to say that many of his theological implications broke out from his desperate experiences. He used the Bible as his entire theological stance and made use of the message of the Bible for transforming the society and he participated in socio-political reformation. Though he draws his materials from the Bible, yet he made use 'Historical Critical Method' and 'Textual Criticism' of the Bible for implementing his biblical hermeneutics. Zairema is not a fundamentalist in the mean time he cannot be regarded as liberal theologian in its full sense, because he was different from other liberal theologians. In the light of his theological implications Zairema can be called scientist-humanist, and anthropologist pastor, as we know from his Biblical approach that Zairema gives humanity supreme importance, also he thought very highly of good relationship among human beings in his theology. As has been discussed throughout the study, it can be seen that realized eschatology is the chief cornerstone in Zairema's theology and in formulating his theology he was deeply influenced by his life experiences. He emphasized that Jesus' salvation includes every sphere of humankind. This is evident from what has been brought out through his entire theological articulations.

Foreword

I feel honoured and privileged to write a foreword to Rev. H. Laldintluanga's book, '*Zairema's Approach to the Bible: A Theological Appraisal*,' on the life and work of Rev. Dr. Zairema, who is one of the greatest figures in the history of Christianity in Mizoram. The book deals with in particular, Rev. Dr. Zairema's contribution on Bible translation into Mizo vernacular, his biblical interpretation and the underlying relevant theological issues.

During his college days, Rev. Dr. Zairema was an exceptionally gifted and brilliant student with penetrating mind, originality of thought and expression. As a person and church leader, he exhibited calmness, humility, simplicity with a respectable quality of leadership. Above all these, he was deeply committed to Christian ethical and moral values as inscribed in the Bible which he believed and urged passionately, should be lived out in the daily life experience of the Christians. His contribution to the church and society in Mizoram had become more significant as he had to take leadership in the Church since the Welsh Missionaries had to leave the country after the Mizos fought for independence from Indian Union in the second half of the 20th century. The Senate of Serampore College (University) awarded him a Doctor of Divinity (*honoraris causa*) Degree for his great contribution for the Church and Society. Among the many important contributions which Rev. Dr. Zairema had made for the church and society, his involvement in the field of Bible translation and interpretation has been of special significance. This was possible due to his mastery in Biblical and Mizo languages, respect for indigenous religio-cultural heritage, openness to the existing wider biblical scholarship and sensitivity to the current contextual realities.

In this book, Rev. H. Laldintluanga, with his sincere research work, has laid bare the various contexts which could have influenced the thought and ideas of Rev. Dr. Zairema, the principles and the impetrative framework which he adopted in his exposition of the Bible. In doing these, the author has carefully analyzed relevant works of Rev. Dr. Zairema with reference to pertinent theological issues, such as, contextualization, liberation and social transformation.

I congratulate Rev. H. Laldintluanga, for publishing this resourceful book with notable skill and commendable scholarship. I wish him a successful career and a fruitful ministry. Finally, I believe and pray that all will be inspired and blessed by God through the reading of this insightful and inspiring book on Rev. Dr. Zairema, whose contribution in the field of Bible translation and interpretation has been both spectacular and reverberating.

Rev. Prof. Vanlalnghaka Ralte
Principal & Professor of New Testament
Aizawl Theological College

Preface

Something of immense importance which is happening in the church today is discovering of the Bible as a gift for faith. We are being driven back to basics in the face of secularization and globalization.

In such a situation, Rev. H. Laldintluanga took up the contextual approach to the Bible for Mizo Christian consideration, because the main focus of this book is about the understanding and interpretation of the Bible by Rev. Dr. Zairema, one of the greatest scholars and theologians among the Mizo Christians who gave so much emphasis on the importance of examining and explaining the Bible in such a way that those who are ministers of God's word may be able to dispense fruitfully the nourishment of the Bible to the people of God. For this purpose, this book '*Zairema's Approach to the Bible: A Theological Appraisal*' served well the need of the hour in one way or the other.

It remains for me to thank the author for this book. The Mizo Christian theological world immensely indebted to him for his enterprise and initiative in the field of Biblical interpretation and theological reflection. It is with great deal of pleasure, I recommend this book to the pastors, leaders of the church and all Christian community who are engaged in reading, examining, interpreting the word of God.

Rev. Prof. Tlanghmingthanga
Professor of Theology and Ethics
Aizawl Theological College

Acknowledgements

First of all, I am very grateful to Almighty God for the uncountable blessings and unfailing love that have been with me all through my theological journey in general and during my thesis writing in particular, who gives me strength and providential care for the completion of my research work. And for granting me the Grace to be here where I am today and especially for letting me know more about Grace through this humble yet heartfelt work.

Lots of people are involved in the completion of this thesis work to whom I am greatly indebted to. First of all, my sincere thanks to my research guide, Rev. Prof. Tlanghmingthanga, who patiently supervised this work. His constant encouragement was a great source of strength. Besides this, I particularly thank him for writing a meaningful preface for this book. I also convey my heartfelt gratitude to Prof. Lalnghakthuami for her interesting suggestions on my research work. The study would not have been completed without their co-operation and constant support.

With a deep sense of gratitude, I acknowledge my indebtedness to Rev. Prof. Vanlalnghaka Ralte, Principal and Professor of New Testament, Aizawl Theological College, who writes interesting foreword message. I will not forgive myself if I do not mention in particular three of my friends Rev. James Lalremmawia, Dr. Royal L. Pakhoungte and Rev. Michael Zorinpuia who went through my drafts, making necessary changes in the grammatical construction and who helped me in my thesis production amidst their busy schedule. I am immensely grateful to them.

I am really grateful to my family for their encouragement, patience and financial support and their unceasing love are my strength. I know that I would not be who and where I am today without the fervent prayers of my beloved mother, the unceasing guidance of my father and the unending love I receive from my brothers and sisters. Moreover, very precious to me is the moral and prayer support which I receive continually from my local church at South Sabual.

Lastly, it is my expectation and prayer that this humble work may be resourceful for getting sights for whoever come across it.

Glory be to God

Date: 2.6.2020 **H. Laldintluanga**

Abbreviations

B. Sc	:	Bachelor of Science
BCM	:	Baptist Church of Mizoram
BD	:	Bachelor of Divinity
BSI	:	Bible Society of India
EATWOT	:	Ecumenical Association of Third World Theologians
KTP	:	Kristian Thalai Pawl
M. Th.	:	Master of Theology (Christian Youth Fellowship)
MCS	:	Mizoram Civil Service
MNF	:	Mizo National Front
MPC	:	Mizoram Presbyterian Church
NCCI	:	National Council of Churches in India
NE/NEI	:	North East / North East India
NEICC	:	North East India Christian Council
NT	:	New Testament
OT	:	Old Testament
PCI	:	Presbyterian Church of India
Ph. D	:	Doctor of Philosophy
PWD	:	Public Work Department
TEF	:	Theological Education Fund
UN	:	United Nations
UT	:	Union Territory
WCC	:	World Council of Churches

Introduction

Methodological Considerations

Focus of the Study

This research work seeks to analyse the main thrust of Zairema's approach to the Bible and his contribution for providing a theoretical framework for social and moral reformation among the Mizo. The Biblicist section of the Mizo populace cannot understand Zairema's interpretation and ideology of translation of the Bible. They seldom understand that Jesus' Salvation is horizontal including socio-eco-political and religion (holistic salvation of humankind) but their understanding is limited only to a vertical ideology like, longing for departure from this miserable earthly life and to live in the place of all pleasures called heaven. Most of the Mizo seldom use the Bible as the rule of faith and conduct in their daily life. Zairema opined that the good relationship between human beings and human beings is the sign of good the relationship between God and human beings. His theological conception revolves around the axis of good relationship between human beings and human beings.

This, however, raises several questions such as: Whether Zairema's theological interpretations are really cherished or not by the Mizo people whose view is dominated by futuristic eschatology, whether Zairema's theology of the Bible is significant for the Mizo Christians or not. And finally, whether Zairema's theology of the Bible is oppressive or liberative.

Important Issues and Methodological Concepts

1) **The Statement of the Problem:** Zairema's approach to the Bible has many distinctions from the approach of the general public for which he was sometimes misunderstood. On the other hand, he was a leading biblical scholar among the Mizo. And it is thus necessary to appraise his approach to the Bible in the light of selected hermeneutical paradigms of the Bible.

2) **Elaboration of the Problem:** Zairema (1917-2008) was the Chief translator of the Mizo Bible and leading Biblical scholar and theologian among the Mizo and an ordained minister of the Presbyterian Church of India (PCI), Mizoram Synod, and he was a pioneer of biblical criticism and a pioneer stimulator of theological debate among the Mizo Christians. Zairema published commentaries on Mark's Gospel, John's Gospel and Genesis for Mizo Adult Sunday School lesson and had written quite a number of articles on the Bible. As he was a translator of the Bible, he himself had a Mizo version of the Bible which is translated fully in accord with his concept. So, Zairema's approach to the Bible and the Mizo traditional understanding of the Bible seem to contradict each other.

Tribal Christians seem to be biblicists who try to use the Bible as a magical book to provide ready-made answers to solve their problems. Mizo Christians also appear to be biblicist in their approach to the Bible. Hence, there is much theological debate among the Mizo Christians about the Bible especially on its authority and the nature of inspiration. Owing to the wrong interpretation and misunderstanding of the Confession of Faith of the PCI article No.1,[1] many Mizo Christians have a wrong conception of the stance of theologians. They often do not consider that it is the book of

[1] Confession of Faith of the PCI article No.1 goes: *The Scriptures of the Old Testament and New Testaments are the Word of God and the Only Infallible Rule of Faith and Duty.*

God's intervention and the history of salvation of humankind. Do the conventional ways of teaching of the Bible as well as the traditional teaching give the people liberative reading of the Bible? Hence, an inquiry and critical evaluation needs to be made on Zairema's understanding of the Bible and the biblicist understanding of the Bible among the Mizo. This study is an attempt to identify which aspects of Zairema's theology of the Bible are significant for the Mizo Christian and which are not. Therefore, this research analyses Zairema's theology of the Bible so as to find its true nature, i.e., whether it is oppressive or liberative?

3) **Previous Researches:** There is a previous research Zairema's contribution on B.D thesis, viz., Zomuansanga Chhangte, *Contribution of Zairema to the church and society in Mizoram,* (2005). However, no post-graduate (or Master) level research has been done so far and the area of problem is quite dissimilar.

4) **The Scope and Limitation:** As indicated above, the study primarily focuses on the prominent Mizo Christian theologian, Zairema's approach to the Bible. A study of other prominent aspects of his thought also made to the extent that these would be helpful to Zairema's theology of the Bible, in the context in which it was developed. Though there will be many liberative reading of the Bible or hermeneutics yet in this book, we are studying Zairema's theology and his interpretation of the Bible. His book and his articles and others aspect to him and his contribution will be omitted deliberately. The research specifically covers the mindset of the Mizos regarding the Bible.

5) **Methodology/Method of Research:** Theological and contextual-liberative method is employed in this study. In order to facilitate this, Zairema's writings, which portray his theology and interpretation of the Bible, are studied. This study is relying much upon library research with the available primary sources and secondary sources of his view. Apart from all available literatures relating to the subject, empirical study in the form of personal interview with some selected figures was held according to necessity.

6) **Structure:** The study is divided into five chapters excluding introduction. The first chapter deals with the historical context of Zairema. It briefly traces Zairema's biographical sketch and Zairema's historical context focusing on social, economic, political and ecclesial context. The second chapter deals with analysis of Zairema's understanding and interpretation of the Bible, focusing on Zairema's work on the Bible such as: i) Translation, ii) Interpretation and iii) Essays on the Bible and Its Related Subjects. This is followed by major features of Zairema's approach to the Bible, concentrating on the four selected areas, namely, the Bible as a Rule of Faith and Duty, Translation Method, Canon and Hermeneutical principles. In the third chapter, we deal with the selected reading paradigms, focusing on Contextual, Liberative, Social Gospel and Transformation aspects. In the fourth chapter we have a theological appraisal of Zairema's understanding of the Bible from the selected reading paradigms. Then in chapter five we conclude the thesis by integrating what have been said in the four major chapters.

Chapter 1

Zairema and His Historical Context

Introduction

Since theology is integrally related to one's own historical context, our first task will be to look at Zairema and his historical context. Hence, in this chapter, a study of Zairema in his historical context will be made: A glimpse of Zairema's life and work and Zairema's historical context. Since Zairema was born on 4th March, 1917 and died on 17th Dec. 2008, his historical context includes from the post British era (from 1890) to today Mizoram context. Therefore, in this chapter we will look at Zairema's Socio-eco-political and ecclesial context from the post British era to the present Mizoram situation.

Zairema's Biographical Sketch

Zairema was born on 4th March, 1918 in Hmunhmeltha village. The original village of his father is Khandaih (Phullen), but because of the Christian persecution in the village they moved to Hmunhmeltha, a Christian village. His father was Doliana, who was a Primary school teacher and his mother was Aibuani. He was brought up by his uncle Mr. Rualkhuma, an Overseer in the local PWD who continued to support him in his study in High School (Shillong) and College (Guwahati), along with he himself earning merit scholarship to meet part of his financial needs. He finished Matriculation (1936) in Govt. High School Shillong, Intermediate of Science (I. Sc. - 1938) and Bachelor of Science (B.Sc.) in First Division from the Cotton College Guwahati under the Calcutta University with Honours (Chemistry) in 1940.[2] He joined Serampore College (University) and secured First Class first in the Bachelor of Divinity (BD) in 1945. He was the first graduate with first class BD degree in that college among the Mizo as well as under the Serampore College (along with Zairema, S. J. Samartha also obtained first class under the United Theological College, Bangalore in 1945).[3] Since he obtained good marks in his BD result, especially Hebrew language, the Principal of Serampore College highly appreciated him and made appreciative comments which goes: "THE CANDIDATE SATISFIED THE EXAMINERS IN HEBREW" by hand writing in his BD certificate.[4]

Rev. C. E. Abraham, the then officiating Principal of Serampore College wrote testimonial letter for Zairem as under:

> Zairema joined the College in July, 1941 but had to abandon his studies early that session for health reason. The following year he came back to the College and read for the BD degree from July 1942 to April, 1945. An Honour graduate in Chemistry (B.Sc) of the University of Calcutta, he secured the unique distinction here of gaining a First Class in the BD. Throughout his Theological course Zairema himself proved to be a most careful student of undoubted intelligence and marked

[2] After he finished B.Sc he served the Headmaster of Middle School as a missionary in the Village of Harasinga among the Kachari, the North Brahmaputra, Assam. His salary was Rs. 35 per month. Zairema, *I Ni Min Pek Hi* (Aizawl: Zorun Community, 2009), 161. (Hereafter will be cited as Zairema, *I Ni Min Pek Hi,*).

[3] *Senate Executive Minute*, 17th June, 1946.

[4] We do not know any other persons who have obtained this kind of Principal's appreciation except Zairema. Zairema, *I Ni Min Pek Hi,* 419.

ability. He was particularly interested in Biblical Studies in which he acquired a competent understanding of the Hebrew and Greek texts prescribed in the course. As a result he obtained the Senators' Prize for Biblical Studies, attaining the unusually high average of 69.6 percent of marks for all his work in these subjects throughout the three years of the examination. In Church History also he stood first in the University of Serampore winning the J. R. Banerjea Prize. Moreover, in Philosophy of Religions he achieved First place, and Second place in the Theology of History and Religions. For his Thesis he wrote on 'The Religion of the Lushais' which secured him the exceptionally high mark of 78 percent and the most appreciative comments of his examiners.

Zairema has the type of personality that command respect and esteem. His quiet efficiency, solid worth, tact, genial humour, and natural dignity will win for him an acknowledged place in any sphere even as they have gained for him the affection and appreciation of his fellow students and the high regard of his teachers. In addition to the influence of an unusually fine character Zairema contributed to the life of the College in a number of ways by the generous exercise of his various gifts. He has musical ability, both vocal and instrumental and was a great asset in his playing for the College services and in the leading of the singing, notably at Hostel prayers. For half of the one session he was Secretary of the SCM Brotherhood and later, for a full session, its President rendering admirable service and displaying his gifts of unostentatious leadership. As Treasurer and subsequently Secretary of 'Codex' he found expression for his literary qualities and produced work well deserving of mention. During the last two months of his stay in College he conducted with great acceptance services of worship for a unit of the WAC(I) stationed at a nearby camp. As a preacher and speaker he has shown powers of thought and resourcefulness along with a conviction and a quiet force fullness in which a certain pleasing humour is frequently noticeable.

Zairema takes a consecrated personality and a well-trained mind of rare quality into the services of the Welsh Presbyterian Church of the North Lushai Hills. He is one for whom the future holds possibilities of Christian Leadership of a high order whether as teacher, preacher, writer, or administrator, in any or all of which he has a vital contribution to make. We wish him well in all that he undertakes and pray for God's guidance and blessing in him and his ministry.

C. E. Abraham
Officiating Principal
On behalf of the Theological Committee
21st July, 1945.[5]

As our knowledge is concerned, we do not know any other persons who have obtained this kind of Principal's appreciation except Zairema.

He married Thangdailovi, daughter of Compounder Chawnga of Dawrpui on March 4, 1947, had three sons and four daughters. He joined Mizoram Presbyterian Church (MPC) Synod and ordained in 1945, and was working half-time in the newly opened Mizo High School. He worked in Mizo High School as a teacher during 1945-1947. He was ordained to the Ministry of Priest for Military service as Chaplain to British army, but war was ended before he joined. He then continued to work as Assistant Headmaster during 1948-1954, when the school was provincialised. He rejoined the Synod in 1954 acting as Honorary

[5] Serampore College, Established 1818, Incorporated by Royal Charter 1827. 'Carey House', Chandernagore. E.I.R Bengal. Rev. G.H.M Angus, MA, DD (on furlough), Officiating President and Registrar of the Senate Rev. C. E. Abraham, MA, BD, Other Members of the Senate Executive: Rev. S. K. Chatterji, MA, Rev. H. I. Frost, MA, STM, Rev. J. F. McFadyen, MA, DD, Rev. C. S. Thoburn, MA, Rev. D. S. Wells, ACA, on 21st July, 1945. Zairema, *I Ni Min Pek HI*, 539-540.

Inspector of Schools, looking after all the schools still managed by the mission till 1959. These were eventually handed over to the Government.

In Barak Valley, just North of Mizoram, the Welsh Mission had been working for more than a century. When the Foreign Missionaries were withdrawn, Rev. Zairema was appointed to take over the on-going works and programmes in 1959. After serving a decade there he was recalled to Mizoram to head the Presbyterian Church as General Secretary in 1968 to 1973 and subsequently as Senior Executive Secretary from 1974-1978. Before his retirement, he worked Bible translation in his residence till his retirement in 1982, when he was at 65 years. After he retired from Mizoram Synod, he carried on literature activities as Chief Translator of Mizo Bible during 1982-1995, then the new translation of the Bible was published in 1995.

The relation between the two communities of Cachar and Mizoram had never been too happy. Cachar provided good headhunting field; Cachar majority population, the Hindus, practised caste rigidly, placing Mizo tribals as lower than the lowest caste. It was with great misgivings that he joined his work whether he would be accepted or rejected. His personal quality, however, won their respect and endearment. His name was even proposed to fill the Town Municipal nominated seat, but before action could be taken, he had to leave the place. Later on, the Bengali speaking Christians were faced with a choice either to be organised as an independent body or merge with some other organisations of North East India (NEI). They decided to merge with Mizo Synod where Rev. Zairema was one of the leading personalities. He was one of the speakers on the first day of National Integration at Silchar. He said to the august gathering, "I cannot lower my high cheekbones nor do you need to perform surgical operation to make your nose like my snub-nose to achieve integration. We cannot do much, but this small thing we can do, we can try to make at least one friend a year from the community other than our own."[6]

---

[6] Zairema, *Ramdom Notes* (Aizawl: Zorun Community, 2009), vii-viii. (Hereafter will be cited as Zairema, *Ramdom Notes,*).

At the initiative of Zairema, the Mizo Presbyterian Church Synod established a number of schools in areas inhabited by the Bru in Mizoram. As a result, large number of Bru can now read and write. He was also one of the originators of the Gospel Mail[7] which was sent to Burma in 1946.

He became prominent leader among Christian circle of NEI. He was Assembly Officer, Silchar (1959-1968), Secretary (1953), Moderator (1959), Member of PCI Trust Committee up to 2006, Executive Committee (1980-1982, 1983-1985), Committee on Evangelism (1980-1982). President of Assam Christian Council (1961-1962), President of the NEICC, 1969-1970, and Executive Committee Member of NCCI. Moderator of Mizoram Synod two times in the years of 1953 and 1973. He represented the United Church of North India at the World Conference of Reformed Churches at Brazil, in 1959.

He served Calcutta and Guwahati University as paper setter and examiner of Mizo Vernacular from 1946 to 1970. He also acted as examiner of the English Paper of the first MCS Examination in 1972.

He served the Government of Mizoram in various capacities such as: Chairman of Arbitration Committee when the political ruling party had serious disagreement with the opposition party; Chairman of the Commission to enquire into the causes of high failure in the High School Leaving Certificate Examination (1975); Member of Planning Board (1975, 1991), Panchayati Raj (1979); Mizo Customary Law (1991); Art and Culture and Mizo Language (1975-1977); Land Tenure (1975-1978); Mizoram Border Investigation Team (1973), Member of Science and Technology (2004) etc.[8]

---

[7] Gospel Mail was one of the revival movements in Mizoram which was a sending of some books from Mizoram to *Zo* people in Myanmar (Burma). Due to the enthusiasm of Evangelist Robuanga that Gospel Mail was organized during 1946-1948. Lalchhuanliana, "Chanchin Tha Dâk Harhna (the Revival Movement of Gospel Mail)," in *Harhna: Mizoram Revival Centenary Souvenir (1906-2006)*, edited by R. L Thanmawia et al. (Aizawl: Synod Revival Committee, 2006), 489.

[8] Zairema was involved in many concerns of Non-Government Organizations (NGOs) and Governmental affairs such as General Secretary Central Young Mizo

He was awarded Doctor of Divinity (*Honoris Causa*) by the Serampore College (University) in 1988 for his contribution in the religious and social life of NEI; Doctor of Literature (*Honoris Causa*) was also awarded to him by the North Eastern Hill University for his varied activities in 1991. His interest was concrete work, design of reinforced concrete buildings such as Church buildings and other private buildings.[9]

Zairema's Historical Context

1) Social Context: The traditional social organization of the Mizos centred around the village.[10] Mizo society is a well-knit society. There is no caste or class system. They participate in all social or religious functions without any consideration of social hierarchy.[11]

The binding ethics of Mizo society which played an important role is *Tlawmngaihna*, The word *tlawmngaihna* is so rich in meaning[12] that it is difficult to render it into one English word. K. Thanzauva, one of the pioneers of NE Indian tribal theologians says, "Many of the definitions... refer to a 'moral code' or 'code of morals'

Association (1946-1947), Councilor, Mizo Union (1947), Vice President Mizo Union(1947) etc. See Zairema, *I Ni Min Pek Hi, xiv-xv.*

[9] Zairema, *Ramdom Note.,* vi-x, and Zairema, *I Ni Min Pek Hi,* xi-xxi, 420-423.

[10] C. Nunthara, *Mizoram: Society and Polity* (New Delhi : Indus Publishing Company, 1996), 64.

[11] S. N. Singh, *Mizoram: Historical, Geographical, Social, Economic, Political and Administrative* (New Delhi: Mittal Publications, 1994), 40.

[12] J. H. Lorain gives a definition in his dictionary. It means: (a) to be self-sacrificing, unselfish, self-denying, persevering, stoical, stout-hearted, plucky, brave, firm, independent, loath to lose one's good reputation, prestige, too proud or self respecting to give it, etc. (b) to persevere, to endure patiently, to make light of personal injuries, to dislike making a fuss about anything; (c) to put one's own inclination on one side and do things which one would rather not do, with the object either of keeping up one's prestige or of helping or pleasing another or of not disappointing another etc. (d) to do whatever the occasion demands no matter how distasteful or inconvenient it may be to oneself or to one's own inclinations; (e) to refuse to give in, give way or be conquered, (f) not to like to refuse a request, to do a thing because one does not like to refuse or because one wishes to please others, (g) to act pluckily or show a brave front. [See J. H. Lorain, *Dictionary of the Lushai Language*, (Calcutta: Royal Asiatic Society of Bengal), 1940].

which are used in a restricted sense of right conduct but in the sense of a principle or philosophical framework, held by a particular community regarding right or wrong relationships with others."[13] Zairema meaningfully gives it a meaning as 'not to be first the bliss and blessing for ourselves but to be first others.'[14]

P. L. Lianzuala says, "*Tlawmngaihna* is a clear and self-evident word representing many qualities and virtues of life."[15] It comprises a wide spectrum of the social virtues such as charity, diligence, patience, bravery, love, kindness, faithfulness and honesty, unselfish sacrifice of one's service to the welfare of the community in all spheres of life. Thus, Challiana beautifully ascribes it as 'the pride and glory of the Mizo people which is a unique possession.'[16] We may, therefore, say that *Tlawmngaihna* is the backbone that upholds the Mizo-ness of the Mizo; the bone marrow in the captives of the community that produces the life-giving cells for the poor, destitute, the widows, the downtrodden and the neglected.[17]

The Mizo family is a 'patriarchal'[18] form of society where linage was traced along the father. As a result, the father of a family is the sole authority in the family. Laughter and merriments in the family

---

[13] K. Thanzauva, *Theology of Community* (Aizawl: Mizo Theological Conference, 1997), 121. (Hereafter will be cited as Thanzauva, *Theology of Community,*).

[14] Zairema, *Thukhawchang Mi Pekte Hi* (Zorun Community, 2009), 207. (Hereafter will be cited as Zairema, *Thukhawchang Mi Pekte Hi,*).

[15] P. L. Lianzuala, "Towards A Theology of Mizo Tlawmngaihna," in *Towards A Tribal Theology The Mizo Perspective,* edited by K. Thanzauva (Mizoram: Mizo Theological Conference, 1989), 55. (Hereafter will be cited as Lianzuala, "Towards A Theology of Mizo Tlawmngaihna,").

[16] Cited by Lianzuala, "Towords A Theology of Mizo Tlawmngaihna," 56.

[17] C. Lalngaihthanga, "A Study of the Theological bases of the Mizoram Presbyterian Church Administrative System," (M.Th. Thesis, Aizawl Theological College, 2009), 17-18. (Hereafter will be cited as Lalngaihthanga, "A Study of the Theological bases of the MPC,).

[18] Gerda Lerner defines 'patriarchy' as the manifestation and institutionalized of male dominance over women and children in the family and the extension of male dominance over women in society in general. It implies that men hold power in all the important institutions of society and that women are deprived of access to such power. It does not imply that women are either totally powerless or totally deprived

were almost absent in every home[19] and the status of women in the early Mizo was not good. N. Chatterji said, "The status of women in society was in no way inferior to that of men and suffered none of those derogatory and discriminatory treatment as may be found in some of the more advanced societies."[20] The Superintendent of the 'Lushai'[21] Hills Major A. G. McCall vividly describes this in his book 'Lushai Chrysalis' and said, "there is little in the Lushai background to disclose the sense of any great chivalry towards woman. Without any ambiguity Lushai has been, and still is, a country for men before it is one for women, or even children. But, where better placed Lushai spare their women the bondage common to the majority, the women retain chorus and grace well into the late years."[22] In fact, this observation and the sayings are prevailing in the present society because man dominates the socio-economic, political and religious affairs and woman plays only the subordinate roles. Due to the introduction of Christianity with education and the subsequent result of modernity the attitude towards woman to a certain extent has been changed.

The Mizo young girls of olden age were very hard working with no time for leisure at all.[23] On the other hand she kept a very low profile in the society as well as in the family where there are some sayings like "A women's word is no word," "Women's wisdom does not reach across the public well," "Fence and wives can be replaced." As a result, husband never helped the wife in domestic affairs because he was afraid to be called *thaibawih*-a henpeck-husband; a man who

---

of rights, influence and resources. See Gerda Lerner, *The Creation of Patriarchy* (New York: Oxford University Press, 1986), 239.

[19] B. Lalthangliana, *Culture and Folklore of Mizoram* (New Delhi: Publications Division of Ministry of Information and Broadcasting, Government of India, 2005), 56 (Hereafter will be cited as Lalthangliana, *Culture and Folklore of Mizoram,*).

[20] N. Chatterji, *Status of Women in the Earlier Mizo Society* (Aizawl: Tribal Research Institute, 1973), 2.

[21] The term 'Lushai' is a name given by the British to refer to the people of Mizoram with a policy 'Divide and Rule,' not a self-imposed term.

[22] A. G. McCall, *Lushai Chrysalis* (Aizawl: Firma KLM Private Ltd. 1977), 26.

[23] Lalthangliana, *Culture and Folklore of Mizoram,* 57f.

is under the thumb of a woman; poetically *thai* is a synonym for woman and *bawih* means 'slave' – slave of woman. However, there was recognition of division of labour among the two sexes of which the degree may differ from the contemporary world.

At the same time the care the Mizo had for widows is noteworthy. They help them in constructing their houses and in clearing the jungles for cultivation. A widow too could have thick forests which are generally fertile for cultivation with the help of fellow male neighbours.[24] They regard the female members of the family as the weaker sex, probably in physical built. In fact, Mizo women occupy a very low status in the family and society. They say, "Crabs and women do not have religions." As a result of that, Mizo women have little or no say in religious, family and social matters.[25]

According to the Mizo custom, family rarely gets together to share their feelings, especially husband and wife did not talk to each other with a smiling face. All the time they were supposed to be serious.[26] A wife never calls her husband by his name, only when a son or daughter is born she addresses him as the father of the child.[27] Meal time is the best time for family's sharing. Father would advise the children and suggest what they do and divides all the work for the family.[28] Therefore, usually they do not visit each other during the meal time and everyone knows that it is a time for the expression of the family's secret.[29]

Children were not given important place in the family. They were not given enough attention by the family. Since, other is busy

---

[24] K. Zawla, *Pi Pute leh an Thlahte Chanchin* (Aijal: The author, 1964), 114.

[25] Lalngaihthanga, "A Study of the Theological bases of the MPC," 15.

[26] V. L. Siama, *Mizo History* (Aizawl: Lengchhawn Press, 1991), 13. Hereafter will be cited as Siama *Mizo History,*).

[27] Sangkima, *Mizos: Society and Social Change* (Guwahati: Spectrum Publications, 1992), 26. (Hereafter will be cited as Sangkima, *Mizos:,*).

[28] Siama, *Mizo History,* 22.

[29] Lalnghakthuami, "A Theological Examination of the Selected Mizo Festivals (Chapchar Kût, Mim Kût and Pawl Kût): Towards a Theology of Mizo Culture" (M.Th. Thesis, United Theological College, 1995), 18. (Hereafter will be cited as Lalnghakthuami, "A Theological Examination of the Selected Mizo Festivals,).

from dawn to dusk and the father did not stay at home most of the time. Hence, no one had enough time for the children. They just grow without parental care and concern. Not only in the family, the society as a whole neglected children from all sphere of life. They considered them to be a bit higher than the animals. There is a saying which states: *Naupang leh Haite chu an piang leh mai a lawm* (Children and *haite*[30] *will continuously produced).*[31]

Early Mizo society was simple and they lived a nomadic life which required selection of new sites for settlements at regular intervals.[32] The political organization was centered round the chief till 1952. The chief administered all matters concerning the village with the help of his council of elders (*Khawnbawl Upa*). The administration of the chief depended upon the ability and foresight of his elders. The *Khawnbawl Upa* were the most important officials in the village and their numbers varied from village to village depending upon the size of the villages. They were appointed by the chief and were liable to be removed at any time by him. However, as chieftainship became hereditary, a chief was succeeded by the eldest or youngest son. The post of *Khawnbawl Upa* was not hereditary in nature, but in some cases, it was made hereditary according to favours received from the chiefs. The responsibility of the chief and his council was to maintain peace and security in village life. When quarrels arose between neighbours, it was the council who settled the problems and restored cordial relations between the two. The Chief and his council also had the responsibility of addressing problems faced by the general public. Thus, the chief and his council were responsible for maintaining peace and security in the village.[33]

---

[30] *Haite* is the name of a species or small gourd; a small ladle made from ground (see, J. H. Lorain, *Dictionary of the Lushai Language*, (Calcutta: Royal Asiatic Society of Bengal), 1940 and, R. K. Ngurchhawna, Z. T. Sangkhuma, Lalzuia Colney, *Zotawng Dictionary* (Aizawl: The Authors, 1997).

[31] Lalnghakthuami, "A Theological Examination of the Selected Mizo Festivals," 18.

[32] Sangkima, *Mizos:*, 60.

[33] Malsawmliana, "Khawnbawl Upa in Early Mizo Society," *Historical Journal Mizoram* VII (November 2006): 41.

2) Economic Context: The traditional economy of the Mizo was mainly based on jhumming cultivation system of agriculture.[34] This system is still the main occupation of majority of the people who are living in rural areas.[35] The Mizo practiced trade and commerce on a small scale with neighbouring states. They practiced barter system of economy. In the olden days, Mizo were economically self-sufficient.[36] The state (Mizoram) has no any economic base such as factory or industry upon which the Mizo people could depend for their economy Although, the Mizo were primarily agriculturists, they depended substantially upon the hunting and domestication of animals such as mithun, pig, dog, fowls, and goat. The mithun was the most valued domesticated animal and wealth was measured on the basis of ownership of mithun. Every family reared pigs as they were frequently used at socio-religious gatherings, and are valued both for their taste and as offerings at religious ceremonies. Other animals that were popular both as food and as sacrificial items, include, goat, dog and poultry. Dogs were also useful for hunting wild animals.[37]

There was a change in Mizoram economy after the British consolidated their rule over Mizoram. Jhumming system of cultivation was still the main occupation of the people. Shifting cultivation was practiced and the staple crops included rice, maize, and millet. Other crops grown were peas, jobs tears, chilies, lady's finger, pumpkin, oil seed, cotton etc., and fruits like cucumber, watermelon, melon and other vegetables.[38]

---

[34] Jhumming cultivation is a kind of primitive way of cultivation in which large areas of forests are cut down, burnt and cleared and cultivated for a year and then abandoned for 4/5 years.

[35] Vardingliani, "Jesus' Concern for the Poor With Reference to Luke 6: 20-21 and Its Implications for the Ministry of Churches" (BD Thesis, Senate of Serampore College, 1997), 48.

[36] J. V. Hluna, "Mizo Society and Economy," in *Mizo Hnamzia leh Khawtlang Nun Siamthat* (Aizawl: Synod Publication Board, 1988), 92.

[37] Malsawmliana, "Megalithic Monuments of Mizoram: A Destructive Study" (Ph.D Thesis, North Eastern Hills University, 2011), 5. (Hereafter will be cited as Malsawmliana, "Megalithic Monuments of Mizoram".

[38] Malsawmliana, "Megalithic Monuments of Mizoram, 5.

Under British administration, there was an attempt to develop the traditional Mizo economy by introducing various economic measures such as the tilling of plains for rice cultivation, promoting and financially assisting the rearing of livestock, planting and cultivation of beverages, fruits etc. During 1908-1909, an agricultural farming complex was established at Chite, a suburb of Aizawl, with a view of demonstrating and instructing the people about the benefits and techniques of crop production.[39] It is recorded that in 1917, the Mizos began sugarcane and coffee plantation and sold the products to the market.[40] Mizoram, then Lushai Hills was directly governed by Governor of Assam during British era. The economic condition of Mizoram was unstable and unproductive during British period.[41]

After India Independence, Mizoram also was governed by District Council from 1952, the large amount of money flowing into Mizoram made some changes in Mizoram economy. The leaders in the District Council's Government as well as the people had never enjoyed and held this kind of large money before. Although, it was intended to benefit all the people, there were a lot of misuses of funds in which many people pocketed as much as they could whereas the rural poor could not get any benefits and other advantages from state budgets in spite of their hard work. Many People feel that this was the beginning of financial corruptions in Mizoram to a large

---

[39] Government of Mizoram, Directorate of Art & Culture, *Mizoram District Gazetteers*, 1989, 113. (Hereafter will be cited as Govt. of Mizoram, Directorate of Art & Culture).

[40] Thangchungnunga, "Mizoram Sumdawnna: Tun Hma leh Tun Hnu," in *Kristiante Rahbi Thar,* edited by Lalchhuanliana (Aizawl: Synod Social Front Committee, 1991), 42.

[41] V. L. Luaia Hranleh, "An Ethical Appraisal of Economic Change in Mizoram 1972-1992" (M.Th. Thesis, United Theological College, 1994), 25. (Hereafter will be cited as Hranleh, "An Ethical Appraisal,). See also Zothantluanga Ralte, "The pace of Socio- Economic and Political Developments: Responses to British Colonialism and the emergence of the Mizo minority nationality in Indian Politics," in *Seminar Papers: International Seminar on Studies on Minority Nationalities of North East India – The Mizos* (Aizawl: Higher and Technical Education, Govt. of Mizoram, 1992), 61.

extent.[42] Overall, in the development plans of the U.T. as well as state of Mizoram, agriculture has been given priority and prime place of attention because the majority of the people have depended on it. At the same time, the government has made great efforts to divert jhumming to settle farming through its various departments. Horticulture development and mechanical tillage is also being given due emphasis. Cultivation of cash crops like tea, coffee, chilly, ginger, cardamom, etc., is also being encouraged and emphasized. Due to the lack of essential infrastructures for development like power and electricity and good communications, the industrial activities had been minimal till Mizoram today. Because of that almost all the needs of Mizoram has been imported from neighboring states.[43] Mizoram has not yet built up a meaningful economy and we are still completely dependent on Central Government.

Several development programmes and poverty alleviation schemes have often failed due to the absence of proper action plan, lack of transport and communications, lack of proper monitoring system etc. Other important and notable reasons for such failures are various kinds of financial corruptions, political favouritism and greed, and lack of skilled and honest human power within the Christian community. If there is no proper check and check's prevention, the existing inequalities of income will be widened, leading to more concentration of wealth in the hands of the high level of government servants pushing down a large number of households below the poverty line.[44]

The state (Mizoram) has no any economic base such as factory or industry upon which the Mizo could depend for their economy. Unproductive jhumming system of agriculture is still the main occupation of the majority of the people in rural areas. While such being the case, the agricultural products of Mizoram are not sufficient to support the people. A huge quality of rice and other essential commodities and goods are imported from other state.

---

[42] Hranleh, "An Ethical Appraisal, 34.

[43] Hranleh, "An Ethical Appraisal, 51.

[44] Hranleh, "An Ethical Appraisal, 7.

3) Political Context: The Mizo history in the 18th and 19th Century is marked by many instances of tribal raids and retaliatory expeditions of security.[45] In 1888-1889, the British dispatched the Chin–Lushai Expedition towards the Lushai hills in order to consolidate their empire in Lushai Hills. By 1890, the British had established their administration at Aizawl and the whole of the Lushai Hills was brought under their administration. The Political Officer was a designated officer in charge of the Lushai Hills with headquarters at Aizawl.[46] The whole tract was divided into northern and southern Hills, with the northern part brought under Assam province while the southern part was placed under the Bengal province. Due to administrative inconvenience, the Chin-Lushai Conference held at Lunglei in December, 1896 recommended the amalgamation of the northern and southern portions into one administrative unit. Accordingly, the Governor-General-in-Council published a notification proclaiming the amalgamation of the two administrative units on April 1, 1898, and the whole of Mizoram was put under the administration of the Chief Commissioner of Assam.[47] The officer in charge of the district was designated as the 'Superintendent', with Major J. Shakespeare as the first Superintendent of the Lushai Hills. Subsequently, the southernmost part of Mizoram, previously called 'The Lakher Hills' was included into the Lushai Hills in 1930.[48] Under the Government of India Act of 1935, the whole of the Lushai Hills was declared an excluded area and then put under the direct administration of the Governor of Assam.[49]

---

[45] "History of Mizoram," MIZRM\History of Mizoram.htm (1Nov 2011).

[46] Foreign Departmental External, Part A, April 1890. Progs. No. 255. *Also see* J. Shakespeare, *Note on the Lushai Hills: Its inhabitants and Its administration since 1888*, No. 1895 J. 29 April 1905, Shillong, 1.cited by Malsawmliana, "Megalithic Monuments of Mizoram:, 3.

[47] Sangkima, *Mizos:*, 3.

[48] Lianhmingthanga, *Material Culture of The Mizo* (Aizawl: Tribal Research Institute, 1988), xi; also see, Thasia T. Azyu, "The System of Administration in South Mizoram With Special Reference to Chhomo Hlychho, Chief of Serkawr 1927-1956," *Historical Journal Mizoram* IV/1 (July, 2003): 18.

[49] Malsawmliana, "Megalithic Monuments of Mizoram:, 5.

It was during the British regime that a political awakening among the Mizo in Lushai Hills started taking shape. The first political party, the Mizo Common People's Union was formed on 9th April 1946. The Party was later renamed as Mizo Union.[50] As the day of Independence drew nearer, the Constituent Assembly of India set up an Advisory Committee to deal with matters relating to the minorities and the tribals. A Sub-Committee, under the chairmanship of Gopinath Bordoloi was formed to advise the Constituent Assembly on the tribal affairs in the NE. The Mizo Union submitted a resolution of this Sub-Committee demanding inclusion of all Mizo inhabited areas adjacent to Lushai Hills.[51]

Following the Bordoloi Sub-Committee's suggestion, a certain amount of autonomy was accepted by the Government and enshrined in the Sixth Schedule of the constitution. The Lushai Hills Autonomous District Council came into being in 1952 followed by the formation of these bodies led to the abolition of chieftainship in the Mizo society.[52] Since India's Independence, the Lushai Hills no longer remained an excluded area, with the coming into force on April 12, 1952 of the Assam Autonomous District (Administration of Justice) Regulation, 1952, with the designations of the

---

[50] Zairema held one of post of the Councillors of Mizo Union in 1947 and Vice President of Mizo Union during, 1946-1947, after he resigned from Mizo Union, Zairema was appointed to be Vice President of *Zalen Pawl* (United Mizo Freedom Organization - UMFO), but he did not accept it [Zairema, *I Ni Min Pek Hi…*, xiv, 267, 272. See also P. Lalnithanga, *Mizorama Politics Inlumleh Chhoh Dan* (Aizawl: The Author, 2008), 28. Chaltuahkhuma, *Political History of Mizoram*, 2nd ed., (Aizawl: Vanthangi, w/o Chaltuahkhuma, 2001,) 76. Before the formation of the Mizo Union, there were voluntary associations, like Young Lushai Association (Y.L.A) R. Vanlawma the then secretary of Mizo Union Party approached the Y.L.A to convert itself into political association. But YLA did not concede to his request and R. Vanlawma, therefore, decided to bring in existence a new political party The Mizo Union. [See J. V. Hluna, "Political Development in Mizoram Since Independence," *Historical Journal Mizoram* VII/1 (Dec, 1997): 12-15].

[51] P. Lalnithanga, *Mizorama Politics Inlumleh Chhoh Dan* (Aizawl: The Author, 2008), 34-38 (Hereafter will be cited as Lalnithanga, *Mizorama Politics,*).

[52] "History of Mizoram," MIZRM\History of Mizoram.htm (1Nov 2011).

Superintendent and Assistant Superintendent changed to Deputy Commissioner and Assistant Deputy Commissioner respectively.[53]

In 1952, the Lushai Hills was given an administrative status i.e. Lushai Hills District Council under the provisions of the Sixth Schedule of the Indian Constitution, having executive, legislative and judicial powers on certain matters. The Lushai Hills District Council and the Pawi-Lakher Regional Council were officially inaugurated by the then Chief Minister of Assam, Bishnu Ram Medhi on April 25, 1952 and on April 23, 1953 respectively. The name, 'Lushai Hills District' was subsequently replaced by 'Mizo District,' with effect from September 1, 1954 by an Act called the Lushai Hills District (Change of Name) Act, 1954 (18 of 1954).[54]

Earlier in 1955, Mizo Cultural Society was formed in 1955 and Laldenga was its Secretary. In March 1960, the name of the Mizo Cultural Society was changed to 'Famine Front.'[55] During the famine of 1959-1960, this society took lead in demanding relief and managed to attract the attention of all sections of the people. The Mizo National Famine Front dropped the word 'Famine' and a new political organization, the Mizo National Front (MNF) was born on 22nd October 1961 under the leadership of Laldenga with the specified goal of achieving sovereign independence of Greater Mizoram.[56] Large scale disturbances broke out on 28th February 1966, government installations at Aizawl, Lunglei, Chawngte, Chhimluang and other places simultaneously. MNF fought an independence from India. The MNF was outlawed in 1967. During 1966 to 1986, Mizoram was a land of commotion.

Then, the Mizo District was again elevated to the status of Union Territory (UT) on January 21, 1972 under the name of Mizoram. On the same day, the UT was officially inaugurated by Ms Indira Gandhi, the then Prime Minister of India. The whole of the territory was divided into three districts viz. Aizawl, Lunglei and Chhimtuipui. The Pawi-Lakher Regional Council was also

[53] Govt. of Mizoram, Directorate of Art & Culture, 54.

[54] Govt. of Mizoram, Directorate of Art & Culture, 54.

[55] Lalnithanga, *Mizorama Politics,* 142.

[56] Lalnithanga, *Mizorama Politics,* 143.

terminated and instead, three autonomous district councils were created for the minority tribes of Chakma, Lakhers and Pawi in the southern part of Mizoram which continue to function till today. After fifteen years, consequent upon the provision of the Constitution (53rd) Amendment Bill and the State of Mizoram Bill (1986), by the Parliament on August 7, 1986, the UT of Mizoram attained full-fledged statehood on February 20, 1987 and became the twenty-third (23rd) state of the Indian Union. The State of Mizoram Bill provided for a 40 member single chamber Legislative Assembly, three districts, nine sub-divisions, three autonomous district councils and village councils.[57] Today, the whole state is divided into eight administrative districts viz., Aizawl, Lunglei, Lawngtlai, Saiha, Champhai, Mamit, Kolasib and Serchhip, with 23 Sub-Divisions.[58]

4) Philosophical and Intellectual Context: Zairema's co-workers in the Church service Lalsawma and Lalngurauva Ralte say that as he was the first B. Sc degree holder among the Mizo, it seems that scientific knowledge severely influenced him for his biblical hermeneutics.[59] C. Rokuma also says that scientists forever content before they could answer the questions of the why, the how and the what. As he has had a science background Zairema tried to answer that questions in his biblical approach especially in the miracles. Seeing as he considered first in his scientific thinking, he was not content after he had finished the questions. Because of that, many people considered him as very liberal.[60] Since Biblical criticism greatly influenced all the theological colleges in the world, Zairema

[57] R. L Thanzawna and C. G. Verghese, *A History of the Mizos,* Vol-II (New Delhi: Vikas Publishing House Pvt. Ltd., 1997), 275.

[58] Malsawmliana, "Megalithic Monuments of Mizoram:, 4.

[59] Interview with Rev. Dr. Lalngurauva Ralte, former Moderator of Mizoram Synod, a close friend and co-worker in the Peace Mission of Zairema, Mission Veng Thlang, Aizawl, 16 December 2011. & and Rev. Dr. Lalsawma, former Moderator and a co-worker in the Peace Mission of Zairema, Mission Veng Thlang, Aizawl, 16 December 2011.

[60] Interview with Elder C. Rokhuma, a close friend of Zairema, Mission Veng Thlang, Aizawl, 12 December 2011.

also found 'Historical Critical Method'[61] and 'Textual Criticism'[62]

---

[61] The historical-critical method investigates the origins of a text and compares them to other texts written at the same time, before, or recently after the text in question. Did other ancient texts, whether biblical or non-biblical, adopt similar forms, use similar ingredients, story-lines, allegories, metaphors and the like. The Historical Critical method focuses on traditionally on questions of sources, dating, authorship, language, genre, history of tradition, historical background, and the history of the reception and interpretation of the text. What do we know of the author and his times? How was he influenced by them? What was his personal story? What other texts did he write and how do they compare what is before us? How does the writing we are studying compare to similar documents of the time? The historical-critical method includes *source criticism, form criticism and redaction criticism.* Besides these *Sociological interpretation,* or socio-scientific criticism, is part of the wider enterprise of historical criticism of the Bible. *Source criticism* "deals with the task of determining the written and oral sources used in the composition of the biblical books as we have them." *Form criticism* "deals with the literary forms which were used in both the written and oral stages of the Bible. It looks for the underlying structures used to convey the subject matter." *Redaction criticism* is "the study of investigating how the individual units of the texts were combined and edited and for what purpose. The redaction critic tries to find theological viewpoints and emphases through the analysis of how the sources were used and combined." {Vanlalnghaka Ralte, *Bible Hrilhfiahna (Biblical Hermeneutics)* (Aizawl: Presbyterian Bible School, 2011), 31. & "Criticism of the Historical-Critical Method of Biblical Scholarship and its Place in Future Exegesis, Historical-Critical Method condemned by Pope St. Pius X – still operative?" http://veneremurcernui.wordpress.com/2012/02/21/historical-critical-method-condemend-by-pope-st-pius-x-still-operative/ (28 Feb 2012).

[62] Zairema, *Kan Bible Hi* (Aizawl: The Author, 2003), 95-112. (Hereafter will be cited as Zairema, *Kan Bible Hi*). Modern methods of textual criticism began to be consolidated from the time of the German Karl Lachmann in the year 1831, with his publication of the Greek text. {See Bruce M. Metzger, *The Text of the New Testament: Its Transmission, Corruption and Restoration* (Oxford: Clarendon Press, 1964), 124. & David Alan Black, *New Testament Textual Criticism: A Concise Guide* (Grand Rapids, Michigan: Baker Academic, 1994), 30}. Then with the publication of *New Testament in Original Greek* by BF Wescott and FJA Hort in 1881, {Kurt Aland and Barbara Aland, *The Text of the New Testament,* translated by Erroll F. Rhodes (Grand Rapids, Michigan: Wm B. Eerdmans Pub. Co. [1987] 1995), 14} there emerged a certain form of critical canon for determining the most likely original readings. The *lower* or *textual* criticism of the Bible starts with the premise that the Bible *is* reliable history. Unfortunately, none of the original Hebrew texts of the Old Testament remain. (Even the Dead Sea scrolls do not qualify, though they come close). The situation with the New Testament is arguably worse, in that no

to be very useful for implementing his biblical hermeneutics. On account of this, many people criticized and condemned him as one who diminished the value of the Bible especially in his commentaries and biblical hermeneutics.

There were so many movements, in the secular and theological realms, not only in the national level, but also in the international scene during Zairema's period. There was a clash between evangelical and liberal groups in the theological circle. And there were political and social movements in the world and Mizoram itself, viz., World War–II, abolition of chieftainship and the uplifting of UT and Statehood from District Council in Mizoram. Zairema says that the translation technique of the Bible was also affected by World War –II, in the form of 'formal equivalent translation' or 'literal translation' to 'Dynamic Equivalent Translation,' especially the effect of bombing of Hiroshima and Nagasaki.[63]

During his college period, immense Indian national consciousness broke out among the Indians. Nationalism and patriotism were encouraged for saving ethnic identity and culture among Indian People. This cultural consciousness also deeply affected all the theological colleges in India. The students and theologians of Serampore College tried to interpret their theologies from the eyes of Indian philosophy and culture. Liberation theology also broke out in that period. This new perspective severely influenced Zairema's theological articulation.[64] Liberation theology influenced Zairema

---

agreement has been possible as to which of the many manuscripts of various New Testament books is actually original. Hence, textual criticism strives to determine which copies of the Old Testament are the most faithful to the original, and which manuscripts of the New Testament are either original (if such can ever be found) or at least faithful and correct. "Biblical criticism," http://creationwiki.org/Biblical_criticism (1 Nov 2011).

[63] The reason of dropping the Atom bomb on these two cities is due to the misinterpretation of the speech of the Prime Minister of Japan. The Aligns group informed Japan to be surrendered, if it is not so, they will use a terrible weapon. The then Prime Minister answered them as "Mokusatsu" which means "we will consider it," but his interpreter interpreted his saying as "we cannot consider it." Then Aligns dropped the Atom Bomb on these two cities. Zairema, *Kan Bible Hi*, 185.

[64] H. Vanlalauva, "Rev. Dr. Zairema'n Chhandamna a Kalpui Dan (Zairema's Theology of Salvation)" in *Rev. Zairema Memorial Lecture Vawi Khatna,* Unpublished

for transforming politics and society. Ever since Zairema came to the belief that the Christian faith has social and political implications, he has been convinced of the need for a relevant ideology to translate faith's vision for society in terms of a political theology. In 1971, he was one of the candidates of Member of Parliament (Lok Sabha).[65]

Zairema's theologies are being shaped by the church and political upheaval of Mizoram. He was arrested and imprisoned by the order of Chalih, the then Chief Minister of Assam during insurgency period of Mizoram. When polices towed him on the street, he thought that the people considered him as one of the convict persons. From that upset situation he found that his famous theology of the cross.[66]

It seems that Zairema was influenced by A. R. H. Mac Donald's[67] political ideology. Mac Donald always found Marxism as a useful ideology in India and attempted to redefine it critically in the light of communist ideology. He did not like to discriminate the rich and the poor and he tried to follow Marxism considering the possibility and necessity of overcoming the present contradictions and suffering. Thus, it seems that Zairema found the importance of political action in order to destroy the exploitative nature of imperialism and capitalism from the society in order to establish a new cultural ethos.[68] Since he admitted some kinds of Marxism, he strongly opined that 'Service to humankind is service to God' during his whole life.[69]

Seminar paper (4th Mar 2011), 7. (Hereafter will be cited as Vanlalauva, "Rev. Dr. Zairema'n Chhandamna a Kalpui Dan,).

[65] Zairema, *I Ni Min Pek Hi,* xiv. In 1957, Zairema had tried to become Member of Parliament (Lok Sabha), Synod Standing Committee also gave permission but he did not file nomination. See R. Lallianzuala, "Kohhrana Rev. Zairema Sulhnu," in *2nd Rev. Zairema Memorial Lecture,* Unpublished Seminar Paper (8th Mar 2012), 29.

[66] Zairema, *Isua Rilru* (Aizawl: Zorun: Community, 2009), 258-259. (Hereafter will be cited as Zairema, *Isua Rilru,*).

[67] Superintendent of Lushai Hills during 1943-1945.

[68] Cf. Zairema, *I Ni Min Pek Hi,* 261-262.

[69] Zairema, *I Ni Min Pek Hi,* 422.

It seems that his BD thesis, "The Religion of Lushais" shaped his theology and occupied one of the corners of his whole life. We can find that he was interested in the primitive religion and culture of Mizo. His research work pressed him to realize the importance of Mizo culture and primal religions. He made use of his discerning the Mizo religion and culture in his Biblical interpretation and in the Bible translation work.[70] As he was 20th century theologian, during his period, so many contemporary theologies were born in the world; such theologies also influenced Zairema for formulating his theological articulations.

5) Ecclesial Context: When the missionaries came, the Mizo readily embraced Christianity. The first two converts among the Mizo *Khuma* and *Khara* got baptized on June 25, 1899.[71] In 1906, the Mizo Christians experienced a great revival. As a result, many people were added to the Church. The second revival was experienced in 1913, the third revival in 1919, and the fourth revival in 1930. One important event early in the third decade 1935 was a new wave of revival. There had been renewal movements – like being born again, consciousness of personal salvation and the like. When we speak of revival in Mizo Church context, it means a new enthusiasm in Church life finding expression not only in words and singing but accompanied by voluntary or involuntary movement of the body.[72] Along with these revival movements, mass conversion occurred through which many people were added Christianity.[73]

Mizo Church had been part of the Khasi Presbyterian Church Assembly. The Presbytery established in 1910 had managed all Church affairs and acted more or less as an independent body but did not have constitutional authority to ordain ministers. The Mizo Assembly, now known as Synod, was constituted in July 1924 at a meeting in Durtlang. Two years later, a constitution to cover all the

---

[70] Vanlalauva, "Rev. Dr. Zairema'n Chhandamna a Kalpui Dan," 5.

[71] J. Meirion Lloyd, *History of the Church in Mizoram* (Aizawl: Synod Publication Board, 1991), 55.

[72] Zairema, *Random Notes,* 78.

[73] V. L. Zaithanga, *From Head-Hunting to Soul-Hunting* (Aizawl: Synod Printing Press, 1981), 15.

Presbyterian Church within the Welsh Mission Fields was adopted with four Synods, each capable of acting independently but linked with each other on certain principles. This also made the Presbyterian Church in NEI a separate body from the Presbyterian Church of Wales. As the Churches were still very young and inexperienced the missionaries continued to play a vital role in the work of the church. The running and the maintenance of schools, hospitals and other institutions continued to remain in their hands but were gradually handed over. The fire of the spirit of giving has to be kept burning without which Christian lives would become stagnant.[74]

Before 1980's, the two churches of Mizoram, viz. Mizoram Presbyterian Church (MPC) and Baptist Church of Mizoram (BCM), had been observing mutual relationships in some respects. They were accepting each other in various levels of ministries and positions in the church. But since 1984 that mutual relationship has been broken due to several serious problems between them.[75] The breakage of mutual relationships between these two big churches affected the solidarity of Mizo society in numerous ways because about 80% of Mizo Christians are the members of these two denominations.[76]

The churches and social voluntary organizations have had a common forum in order to respond to socio-economic and political issues in Mizoram. Since most Mizo are Christians, the church has been one of the most influential bodies in Mizoram.[77]

Conclusion

In the light of above the points, the British annexation and the advent of Christianity had profound effect on Mizo socio-economic, political and religio-cultural life. They were also led by an institutionalized Church which plays great role in shaping the

---

[74] Zairema, *Random Notes,* 77, 78.

[75] *Mizoram Presbyterian Kohhran Synod Bu Vawi 60-na (Minutes of 60th Synod Meeting)* (Aizawl: Synod Publication Board, 1984), 169-173, cited by Hranleh, *An Ethical Appraisal,* 64.

[76] Hranleh, "An Ethical Appraisal, 64.

[77] Hranleh, "An Ethical Appraisal, 70.

moral and ethical values of the people. Zairema experienced many incidents in socio-economic, political and religious upheavals in India and Mizoram. All of the historical contexts play an important role for the implications of Zairema's theology.

Chapter 2

Analysis of Zairema's Understanding and Interpretation of the Bible

Introduction

In our study of the historical context, our first concern is to have a glimpse of Zairema's life and work. Biblical concerns shaped Zairema's whole life. He wrote Biblical commentaries and many articles for interpretation and instruction of the Bible. He was involved in Mizo Bible translation during and after his retirement from the ministry in the church. Therefore, in this chapter we will discuss Zairema's understanding and interpretation of the Bible as given below:

Zairema's Work on the Bible

1) Translation: Zairema's famous involvement was in Bible translation. In the Mizo Bible translation, the New Testament (NT) was completed and published in 1917, re-edited in 1924, serving the church for the next sixty years or more. The task of translating the Old Testament (OT) was also jointly undertaken under the auspices of the BSI. The same procedure as followed in the NT was followed. The books were framed out to translators. The translation work was disrupted by the outbreak of the Second World War (1939-1945). When the War was ended, the North (MPC) and the South (BCM) expanded their respective translation committees. In the North, by the year 1947, Rev. Liangkhaia was transferred from Saitual to Mission Headquarters at Aizawl to be in-charge of 'Literature and Translation.' Rev. Liangkhaia then translated the rest of the OT books which were assigned to the North such as: Job, Ecclesiastes, Song of Songs, Jeremiah, Lamentations, Ezekiel, Daniel, Zechariah, Zephaniah, Haggai, Habakkuk and Malachi. Three member editing groups were formed to look into the drafts made by Rev. Liangkhaia, such as, (1) Rev. J. M. Lloyd (leader), Mr. Muka (Synod Evangelist) and Rev. Chhuahkhama; (2) Rev. B. E. Jones (Leader), Rev. Liangkhaia, Elder Ch. Pasena and Elder Vanchuanga; 3) Rev. Saiaithanga, Rev. Thanga and Rev. Zairema.[78]

The BSI compiled the Mizo OT and the 6th Edition of the Mizo NT (1950) into a single volume and printed the first Mizo Bible in 1959.[79] In this first translation work, especially in the OT, Zairema was one of the translators of Mizo Bible, he participated from the translation of OT portion of the Old Version of Mizo Bible from 1947. With the permission of the BSI authority minor re-editing work was done on the First Mizo Bible by a team of scholars from the North and the South in which about 900 items were changed.[80] This re-edited version was published in the Synod Press in 1982. First it was published as the Pulpit Bible, and then a standard size was published from the same text. In this re-editing group, Zairema was appointed as Secretary of re-editing group of Mizo Old Version and Translation Group.[81] He was a Chief Translator from 1982-1996 after he retired from the Mizoram Synod church's official activities.

---

78 Zairema, *Kan Bible Hi*, 177.

79 Vanlalnghaka Ralte, "A Brief History of Mizo Bible Translations," *Mizoram Journal of Theology* II/1 (Jan.-June 2011): 80. (Hereafter will be cited as Vanlalnghaka Ralte, "A Brief History of Mizo Bible Translations,").

80 Zairema, *Kan Bible Hi*, 190.

81 Zairema, *Kan Bible Hi...*, 188. {In this re-editing group, the appointed members were: *From the South* (Baptist Church of Mizoram), Rev. Zathanga, Rev.

The translation committee was formed from the names recommended by both the Assembly of the BCM (South) and the MPC (North). The members were: From the South 1) Rev. C. L. Hminga, 2) Rev. H. S. Luaia, 3) Rev. Raltawnga, 4) Rev. K. Thangchungnunga, 5) Rev. Chalbuanga and 6) Ms. R. L Hnuni. From the North – 1) Rev. Lalbiaktluanga, 2) Rev. C. Pazawna, 3) Rev. Lalngurauva Ralte, 4) Rev. V. L Zaithanga, 5) Rev. Zaihmingthanga 6) Rev. C. Ronghinga, and 7) Rev. Zairema. As Zairema got retired from active service of the MPC in 1982, the BSI appointed him to be full time worker in the translation works and designated him as 'Chief Translator' in the New Mizo Bible translation project. In the meantime, by April 1983, the BCM also designated Rev. Chalbuanga to be a fulltime worker in the same project to work side by side with Rev. Zairema. The salaries of both the translators were equally borne by the BSI and their respective churches. The Translation Committee members were assigned portions of the Bible to be translated. The drafts would be submitted to the Chief Translator who would in turn read and return to the translators with critical comments. Then after the revised drafts had been received from the translators they would be placed before the committee. The final drafts of the NT translation were completed by 1984 for trial print.[82]

A new committee was formed for the OT translation which comprised of the following members: From South- (1) Rev. H. S. Luaia (2) Rev. C. L. Hminga, (3) Rev. Raltawnga, and (4) Rev. Sangchema, and (5) Rev. Chalbuanga. From the North – (1) Rev. Zairem (2) Rev. Lalbiaktluanga (3) Rev. Lalchhuanliana, (4) Rev.

Challiana, Rev. H. S. Luaia, Rev. C. L. Hminga, Rev. Thangchungnunga and *from the North* (Presbyterian), Rev. Liangkhaia, Rev. J. M. Lloyd, Rev. Saiaithanga Rev. Pazawna, Rev. V. L. Zaithanga, Rev. Zairema, Mr. Muka. Rev. Zairema, who was staying in Silchar was appointed as the Secretary of Translation Group, (Zairema, *Kan Bible Hi,* 187-188)}.

[82] Vanlalnghaka Ralte, "A Brief History of Mizo Bible Translations," 85-86. Rev. Dr. H. S. Luaia also said, "After we finished the Bible portions which we translated in the day time, Zairema typed it all by typewriter in the same night. He was very industrious." Interview with Rev. Dr. H. S. Luaia, one of the Bible Translation Members, at his residence Ramzotlang, Lunglei, 20th April, 2011. Zairema typed through the Bible around three times by typewriter, *Kan Bible Hi*..., 199.

Thansiama, (5) Rev. Z. T. Sangkhuma, (6) Rev. Lalthanga, (7) Rev. Lalruma. Since it was found that the translation work could not progress much with members working on part-time basis, a core Translation Committee was formed to work on full-time basis which comprised of five members namely, Rev. Zairema, Rev. Lalthanga, Rev. Lalruma, Rev. H. S. Luaia and Rev. Chalbuanga. Then the Old Testament was completed in 1992,[83] and a new version (Contemporary Version) was released on November 25, 1995 by Dr. A. M. Prabhakaran, Director, i/c Translations, BSI.[84] Unfortunately, there were serious printing mistakes particularly relating to the deletion of the occurrences of a controversial Hebrew word "Selah" in the Book of Psalms, the computer accidentally deleted all the Mizo word 'sela' along with 'Selah.' A re-edited version was published in 2007. More recently, the latest re-edited version of the Mizo Holy Bible (Contemporary Version- C.V) was done in 2010 and is expected to be ready soon for the Mizo Bible readers.[85] As he was a translator of the Bible, he also translated the Apocrypha to Mizo in 1989[86] and he himself had a Mizo version of the Bible which is translated fully in accord with his concept. His Bible was published for his family members and close friends alone.

2) Interpretation: As P. R. Hmuaka, a Mizo NT Scholar, regarded him as 'Father of Mizo Biblical Criticism,'[87] Zairema has

[83] Zairema, *Kan Bible Hi*, 199.

[84] "Milestone of the Aizawl Auxiliary: 1st June, 1978-1st June 2003" in *Mel Lung, Auxiliary Silver Jubilee Souvenir,* 133, cited by Vanlalnghaka Ralte, "A Brief History of Mizo Bible Translations," 87.

[85] Vanlalnghaka Ralte, "A Brief History of Mizo Bible Translations," 87. (In this re-editing, Bible Society of India appointed Rev. V. Lalzawnga to make rectification of the New Bible translation. While making correction, Rev. Zairema and Rev. H. S. Luaia are not content as they opined that Rev. V. Lalzawnga did not know the milieu of translation work and he made a correction according to his own will. {See Zairema, *Thian Lehkhathawn* (Aizawl: Zorun Community, 2009), 13, 68, 72. (Hereafter will be cited as Zairema, *Thian Lehkhathawn*). And Interview with Rev. Dr. H. S. Luaia, Zairema's friend and one of the translator members, at his residence Ramzotlang, Lunglei, 20 April, 2011.}.

[86] R. Lallianzuala, "Kohhrana Rev. Zairema Sulhnu," in *2nd Rev. Zairema Memorial Lecture,* Unpublished Seminar Paper, 8th Mar. 2012, 17.

[87] Zairema, *I Ni Min Pek Hi,* 428.

had a strong conviction for Biblical hermeneutic. He never hesitated to use liberal approach for interpreting the Bible. When we read carefully his Bible commentaries, we can easily grasp that he was a man of great intelligence advance in theological education, especially in Biblical criticism. He published commentaries on Gospel of Mark and John the Gospel and Genesis (a selected text from Genesis) for Mizo Adult Sunday School lesson.

We will look at his works as under:

a) *Genesis Bu Thlanchhuah Hrilhfiahna (Commentary on selected texts from Genesis):* Among Zairema's written books this is the first one written in 1957 to be used as the text book of Adult Mizo Sunday School for the year 1958.[88] In this book, Zairema picked out some important texts between chapters 1 to 45 and added one lesson 'Christian couple.' He frankly introduced his perspective in the introductory notes. He strongly opined that the book of Genesis is impossible to accept literally. There are so many indefinable portions in the book. We should learn as not to be historical fact but to be the record book for the study between the relationship God and human being.[89]

b) Chanchintha Marka Ziak Hrilhfiahna (A commentary on the Gospel of Mark): Zairema wrote a Commentary on Mark in 1970 for adult Sunday school lesson for studying in 1971. This book provoked some negative responses. He strongly asserted his opinions about the book of the Gospel of Mark. He used the 'Historical Critical Method' of Biblical criticism. Most of the Mizo Christians could not digest his interpretation, they harshly condemned and blamed him saying, "Rev. Zairema is not a born again person, he will not enter into heaven."[90] Evan. Robuanga, a close friend of Zairema

---

[88] H. Remthanga, *Mizoram Presbyterian Kohhran Synd Thurel Lak Khawm*, Vol.-II (1951-1970) (Aiawl: Synod Literature & Publication Board, 1998), 122.

[89] Zairema, *Genesis Bu Thlanchhuah Hrilhfiahna* (Aizawl: Jubili K. T. P Br. Mission Veng, 1998), ii, iv. (Hereafter will be cited as Zairema, *Genesis,*). This book was reprinted by Jubilee KTP Branch, Mission Vengthlang in 1998 with a hope that it would be helpful for "Genesis Hrilhfiahna," the Adult Sunday School Text book of 1998.

[90] This condemnation phrase is very popular in 1970s in Mizoram. See also Chuauthuama, "Theological Education in Mizoram Retrospect and Prospect" in

also said, "Zairema used to write his thoughts frankly and for that reason many people could not appreciate his books. He never made reservation, and did what he wants without hesitation. For this reason his commentary on Mark was also criticised negatively by many Churchgoers"[91] However, Zairema explained that every commentary is the interpretation of the writer. It is not to be accepted as the Church's official teaching. It is written to aid the Bible Society.[92]

c) *Chanchintha Johana ziak hrilhfiahna (A Commentary on John's Gospel):* Zairema wrote another commentary, it was a commentary on John's Gospel written in 1974. He used liberal approach for his biblical hermeneutic in this book also. But if we compare with the commentary of Mark' Gospel, we can see that the commentary of John is smoother than that of Mark. Though Zairema did not change his stand on interpreting the Bible, yet perhaps because of that, Church members also did not give negative comment. Zairema also comments upon this latter commentary, saying "when I wrote a commentary on Mark there were some negative comments. Later I wrote a commentary on John, but no one was mentioning any negative comment. It was amazing."[93]

3) Essays on the Bible and Its Related Subjects: Zairema wrote quite a number of articles on the Bible, namely, 'the Techniques of Bible Translation,' 'Authority of the Bible,' 'the Bible in Mizo,' 'Bible Translation in North East India,' 'Bible *Lehlin*-I & II (Bible Translation –I & II),' 'Bible *Lehlin Chungchang* (Notes on Translation of the Mizo Bible),' 'Bible *Lehlin leh Thurin* (Bible Translation and Doctrine),' 'Bible *Thusawi* (literally means, The Sayings of the Bible*),' 'Pathian, Rethei Lam Awn* (God of the poor),' '*Inthawina (Bible lehlinah*) (sacrifice, in the Mizo Bible),' '*Mizo Bible-a Alkatra* (Bitumen in the Mizo Bible),' '*Engkim Lalpa* (YHWH Shaboath).' Besides these, he published *Kan Bible Hi,*

Kal Hmasate Hlutna (Aizawl: The Author, 2009), 138.

[91] Cited by Zomuansanga Chhangte, "Contribution of Zairema to the Church and the Society in Mizoram" (B.D. Thesis, Aizawl Theological College, 2005), 35. (Hereafter will be cited as Chhangte, "Contribution of Zairema,).

[92] Chhangte, "Contribution of Zairema, 36.

[93] Cited by Chhangte, "Contribution of Zairema, 36.

(This Bible of Ours). In this book, he wrote about the Bible from its origin and the translation work from the beginning in the world and he told us that so many translation techniques and authority of the Bible and an indication of the Bible which was to be read and accepted. Since he explained many theological debatable issues, we can see Zairema's hermeneutical principle in this book.[94]

Major Features of Zairema's Approach to the Bible

1) The Bible as a Rule of Faith and Duty: In the Confession of Faith of the PCI, article No.1 goes: *The Scriptures of the Old Testament and New Testaments are the Word of God and the only infallible rule of faith and duty.*[95] *Owing to the wrong interpretation and misunderstanding of the Confession of Faith of the PCI, many Mizo Christians have a wrong conception of the stance of theologians. Zarema tried to specify the meaning of the 'the only infallible rule of faith and duty.'* According to him, the Bible is the authoritative of rule of faith and duty but at the same time he did not accept the verbal inspiration. He clearly argued about 'the rule of faith and duty' in his books, he says that the basic foundation of the doctrine and theology is taken from the teaching of Jesus, which is followed by other NT's authors. If there is no reliable norm for the rule of faith and conduct in Jesus' word and in the Bible itself, we base the tradition of the elders. If there is no tradition of the elders again, we use the voice of the assembly of the church and the words of God which are revealed in the mind of the Church members.[96] Besides this, he mentioned clearly while he was trying to stop a debate about infallible and inerrancy of the Bible, he utters, "it is not the most important to say that 'the Bible is infallible and inerrancy,' but it is sufficient to say that 'the Bible is the Word of God.' For the Roman Catholic Church, the word of the

---

[94] The Mizo academy of Letters (M.A.L) selected this book as Book of the Year 2003, signifying that it is the best book that is in publication during the year 2003. The M.A.L. offered him award on 23rd April, 2004 (Friday). This award carries citation and cash prize of Rs. 5,000.00 plus one year free subscription of the monthly magazine *Thu Leh Hla*.

[95] *Manual of Worship of the Presbyterian Church of India* (Shillong: The Presbyterian Church of India, 2002), 125-126.

[96] Zairema, *Genesis*, viii.

Pope (Papal Bull) is infallible and for the MPC the resolution of the Synod meeting is infallible. Firstly we should accept it, but if it is not relevant we will change in the next meeting."[97]

When we look at Zairema's understanding and interpretation of the Bible, he was very much concerned with realizing the real meaning and the main message of the word of God. It seems that he rejected both radical conservative and modernist-liberal approach of the Bible, but at the same time, it seems that he eliminated narrow view of the Bible. He opined that there is no personal development only from conservative approach.[98] He used to say that there is no maturity without accommodating liberal approach.[99]

2) Translation Method: The earlier versions of Mizo Bible were chiefly based on King James or Revised Version rather than the texts of both Hebrew and Greek. Zairema wrote about the Mizo translation method in his articles viz. 'Bible Translation in NEI,' 'The Bible in Mizo' and in his popular book 'Kan Bible Hi.' Even if those missionaries responsible for the project were well versed in the original languages their products showed their great dependence on the English versions. The principle of translation they followed is now known as 'formal equivalent translation' or 'literal translation.' Every attempt was made to consistently translate the same original word into the same word once used in the receptor language, although the word might have different meaning in another context.[100] Zairema has indicated the early method of Mizo Bible translation mentioning:

> Every word whether it has significant meaning or not is translated and so there are lots of ands, beholds etc. Sentence construction and clause forms were often reproduced. Only half-hearted attempts were made to split the more involved sentences into simpler sentences, because a verb or some other word has be repeated or introduced which were not in English. Great care was taken to indicate qualifying words that must be used

[97] Zairema, *Kan Bible Hi,* 239.

[98] Zairema, *Kan Bible Hi,* 8.

[99] Zairema, *Kan Bible Hi,* 8-9, 218.

[100] Zairema, *Ramdom Notes,* 42. & *Kan Bible Hi,* 179.

> in the receptor language but which was implicit in the original and printed in italics. Passive forms were introduced into tribal language where such forms are rare. Rhetorical questions were reproduced in the same form where a straight forward sentence from would be easier to understand.[101]

When the BSI adopted the new method of translation namely the usage of a language used by common people called common language and the use of dynamic rather than formal equivalence, NT of the Bible in Mizo was also undertaken.[102] In the year 1960s there was a felt need to revise more thoroughly the Old Version (O.V.) of the Mizo Bible. Some initial works had been done by scholars from both North and the South. But, as the BSI had been adopting a new method of translation under the banner of 'dynamic equivalent' translation method, it was finally decided to undertake a new translation project instead of revising the old one. The BSI provided more updated materials for Bible translation work, organized trainings for the translators, and even the new English version, namely, The Good News Bible (Today's English Version) which had became the basis for the new Mizo Bible translation was also available then.[103]

Like King James Bible, the Bible transformed Mizo lives giving them new motives for living. Zairema clearly mentioned the method what they use for the new version of Mizo Bible, he says, "In the new translation, we try to put God's words in a language even children, women and men in the market can understand."[104]

3) Canon: Etymologically, the word 'canon' comes from the Greek word *'Kanon'* which was derived from a Semitic root word, Hebrew *'qaneh,'* Assyrian *'qanu'* Akladian *'qin.'* It passed into Greek as *'kanna'* or *'kane,'* into Latin as *'canna'* and then to English as 'cane.' It originally meant 'reed' (English 'canon') and came to mean

---

[101] Zairema, *Ramdom Notes,* 42.

[102] Zairema, *Random Notes*, 123-124.

[103] Vanlalnghaka Ralte, "A Brief History of Mizo Bible Translations," 84-85.

[104] Zairema, *Random Notes*, 124-125.

something firm and straight.[105] It was eventually used to mean 'rule' or 'standard.' The term 'canon' can have various meanings in the field of music, art and literature, etc. The term 'canon' when used with reference to the Bible means the collection of the books which are received and accepted as divinely inspired and authoritative for faith and life.[106]

Zairema wrote about the significance of canonization as 1) If we accept all the good number of religious books for the Bible, it will be much more and the selection of that good books cannot be similar. Therefore, canon of the Bible is very decisive. 2) The chosen text for the Bible will be stable and unchangeable. It cannot be said

---

[105] James A Sanders "Canon," *Anchor Bible Dictionary* Vol. – I, edited by David Noel Freedman et al. (New York: Doubleday, 1992), 832. During the days of the early Church a good number of religious books were written by various persons. So with the emergence of false teachings like the Gnostic teachings, Marcion canon etc there were questions concerning the divine authority of the writings, some of which were accepted by the Church and others rejected by the Church. Merill F. Unger "Canon of Scripture," *Ungler's Bible Dictionary* (Chicago: Moody Press, 1975), 174. Although there were no considerations of having the Canonical New Testament when the Early Church were established and the Old Testament were used as Scriptures and oral tradition still in practice, later, with time and because of the various problems as mentioned above and others as well the regulations so written became normative for Christians and moreover it was necessary to separate Scripture from religious literatures. Neil. R. Lightfoot, *How We Got The Bible* (Secunderabad, Andhra Pradesh: OM Books, 2005) 109. The formation of the Jewish canon was hundreds of years in process. The oldest portion of the Pentateuch is regarded by some as having been written in the ninth century B.C. and by others as early as the fourteenth. Some regard the latest portions to be the postexilic prophets written in the fifth century B.C., while others consider Daniel to be as late as the second century B.C. The book of Psalms seems to reflect this extremely long process of canonization spanning a thousand years from the Psalm attributed to Moses (Ps 90) to that written during the Babylonian exile (Ps 137). It is significant that the people later called Israel do not claim to have produced any writings from the time of Abraham to that of Moses, although we now know that writing existed in highly sophisticated form since before the time of Abraham (as the recently discovered Ebla tablets have shown). See John R. McRay, "Canon," *The Dictionary of Bible and Religion*, edited by William H. Gentz (Nashville, Tennessee: Abingdon Press, 1986), 177-178.

[106] Bruce M Metzer, *The New Testament, Its Background, Growth, and Content* (London: Abingdon Press, 1969), 273.

that the selected portion is whether relevant or not for the particular context. 3) Bible is the criterion and our dependence for our moral and social ethics, so it will be reliable and unchangeable.[107] Zairema mentioned in detail about the origin of the Bible and the process of canonization in his book *Kan Bible Hi.* It seems that Zairema did not like to close canon of the Bible and he even questioned the necessity of closing canonization.[108]

4) Hermeneutical Principles: The word hermeneutics is derived from Greek *hermeneutike* via New Latin *hermeneutica*, the art of interpretation. In its verbal form *hermeneuo* means "to interpret," "to expound," "to explain," that is to translate what has been spoken or written in a foreign tongue into the vernacular.[109] Richard Solen defines "Traditionally, Hermeneutics sought to establish the principles, methods, and rules needed in the interpretation of written texts, particularly sacred texts whose literal meaning was in doubt or had become unbelievable because of the shifting world views or deepening moral sensitivity, and thus required interpretation in order to be preserved as sacred literatures."[110] Carl Braaten sees hermeneutics as "the science of reflecting on how a word or an event in the past time and culture may be understood and become existentially meaningful in our present situation."[111] For Tate, "Hermeneutics in the broad sense is bipolar: exegesis and interpretation."[112]

---

[107] Zairema, *Kan Bible Hi*, 23.

[108] Zairema, *Kan Bible Hi*, 38-39.

[109] *A Greek-English Lexicon of the New Testament,* translated and enlarged by J. M. Thayer (New York: American Book Company, 1889), 250 It is used in this sense in Xenophon's Anabasis (5,4,4) in about 400 B.C. Its cognate's *hermeneia, hermeneus, hermeneutes,* etc. are used in a variety of senses in both Greek-classics and *koine.*

[110] Richard N. Soulen, *Handbook of Biblical Criticism* (Atlanta: John Knox: Press, 1976), 73.

[111] Carl Braaten, *History and Hermeneutics* (Philadelphia: Fortress Press, 1966), 131.

[112] W. Randolph Tate. *Biblical Interpretation: An Integrated Approach,* 3rd ed. (Peabody, Massachusetts: Hendrickson Publishers, Inc., [1991, 1997], 2008), 1. Exegesis is the process of examining a text to ascertain what its first readers would

The main features of Zairema's biblical hermeneutical principles are as follows:

1) *The Bible is the book of the revelation of God:* According to Zairema, The Bible is the book of revelation of God. It is not the book of the study of universe, science, history and anthropology, but God revealed Godself to human beings through Word.[113] That God's words are proclaimed by the chosen people of God, e.g. prophets etc. God' revelation was received by human beings in their own distinctive language and culture. He said, "God spoke to every nation with a no-language language. That is how he (sic) often continues to speak to us…People with rich vocabulary are likely to understand the message in a more manner and can express it in a more forceful way, like poets do."[114] So, to Zairema, when we interpret the Bible, we should remember that imperfect human being received the Word of God imperfectly and proclaimed it improperly too. At the same time, the will of God is possible to know clearly from the messages.[115]

2) *Biblical interpretation should be contextualized:* Koyama defines contextualization as a two step process, "*First,* to articulate Jesus Christ in culturally appropriate, communicatively appropriate words; and *second,* to criticize, reform, dethrone, or oppose culture if it is found to be against what the name of Jesus Christ stands for."[116] Zairema's biblical hermeneutics is also contextual and indigenous. To him, the Gospel must be understandable, but in its full reality. He used to say that our preaching and interpretation of the Bible have often been in terms unnatural to Mizo but to be natural Mizo expression.[117] He opined that Mizo should learn to express some Biblical words according to their natural expression, for instance, the word we use is for righteousness is *Felna* which fails, after so many

have understood it to mean. Interpretation is the task of explaining or drawing out the implications of that understanding for contemporary readers and hearers.

[113] Zairema, *Kan Bible Hi*, 229.

[114] Zairema, *Random Notes*, 15.

[115] Cf. Zairema, *Kan Bible Hi*, 229-230.

[116] "Waterbuffalo theology," http://sites.google.com/site/eggen4jc/waterbuffalo theology (17Aug 2011).

[117] Zairema, *Random Notes*, 17.

years of use and explanation, to convey the courtroom language of the original. This, of course, is the job of translators which is being rectified in the new translation. It is the task of theologians to convey this into natural Mizo.[118]

3) *To be interpreted from the root meaning:* It seems that Zairema used the narrative, grammatical and form critical approach in his biblical hermeneutics. He used to say that not only to take out the only one verse or one sentence but to study from the whole message of the chapter or from the light of the whole messages of the Bible.[119] He gave a meaningful example for that, in the time of Paul, they did not think that practicing slavery was not the will of God. The writing skill of the authors of the Bible is not similar. Some authors were highly educated whereas some authors did not have good writing skill and they wrote whatever they received the word of God in their level best. That record book of the word of God is our Bible.[120]

Conclusion

In the analysis of above the points we can identify that Zairema makes use liberal approach and "Biblical Theology"[121] for his biblical hermeneutics. Since liberation theology motivated him in

---

[118] Zairema, *Random Notes*, 17.

[119] Zairema, *Lehkhabu Tê Pasarih* (Aizawl: Zorun Community, 2009), 16. (Hereafter will be cited as Zairema, *Lehkhabu Tê Pasarih…*,).

[120] Zairema, *Kan Bible Hi*, 229, & Zairema, "*Lehkhabu Tê Pasarih*, 16-17.

[121] Biblical Theology came into beings in 1940-1950 from the North America. In the beginning, it was a theology for against liberalism and Neo-orthodoxy. Biblical theologians seek not only the biblical texts convey theological ideas but they regard to normatively for the church today. [Gareth Jones, ed., *The Blackwell Companion to Modern Theology* (Oxford: Blackwell Publishing Ltd., 2007), 23]. Biblical Theology, according to G.E. Ladd, is *theology*: it is primarily a story about God and God's concern for human beings. It exists only because of the divine initiative realizing itself in a series of divine acts whose objective is human redemption. Biblical theology therefore is not exclusively, or even primarily, a system of abstract theological truths. It is basically the description and interpretation of the divine activity within the scene of human history that seeks humanity's redemption. George Eldon Ladd, *A Theology of the New Testament* (Grand Rapids, Michigan: William B. Eerdmans Publishing Company, revised edition [1947], 1993), 21.

his theological articulations, Zairema was very much concerned with the role of Biblical Theology for social dimension and he wanted to change the Mizo approach to the Bible that it should be praxis oriented and not merely spiritual in orientation. His approach to the Bible contributed to providing a theoretical framework for social and moral reformation among the Mizo. He found the Bible to be very useful for transforming society and he involved himself for reforming the political and social life driven by his understanding of the word of God and his understanding of what Jesus' salvation means to human beings. He used the Bible as his entire theological stance and made use of the message of the Bible for transforming the society and he participated in socio-political reformation.

Chapter 3

Selected Reading Paradigms

Introduction

Although we will study Zairema's biblical approach in the light of some selected reading paradigms of the Bible, his particular approach will be studied in the later chapter. Since we will study about Zairema's Biblical approach in the light of some selected reading paradigms, the basic meaning and approaches of such paradigms need to be introduced first. Therefore in this chapter, we shall deal with Contextualization, Liberative, Transformation and Social Gospel for the selected reading paradigms.

Contextual

James Cone's thought, along with Paul Tillich, stresses the idea that theology is not universal, but tied to specific historical contexts.[122] After World War II (1939 to 1945), the end of the colonial era

---

[122] "Black Theology Liberation Ethics-Society," http://www.amazon.com/Black-Theology-Liberation-Ethics-Society/dp/0883446855/ref=cm_cr_pr_simst (15 Aug. 2010).

brought independence to many nations. This unleashed new social, economic and political power which are radically affecting the lifestyle of the people of these nations.[123] Christians in these countries started searching for self-identity. They began to look at what they have inherited as the gospel message and Christian culture. They became aware of the need to own the gospel a new in their own culture, and express it in an idiom and concept that make sense to their people.[124] From that time onwards, accommodation or adaptation was developed in the Roman Catholic circle; and the concept of indigenization was developed among the Protestant.[125] The primary concerned of these developments was indigenizing the method of evangelism, forms of worship, social customs and church architectures.

The word 'contextualization' was first coined by *Shoki Coe* and *Aharon Sapsezian*, Directors of the Theological Education Fund (TEF) of WCC in their report 'Ministry in Context' in 1972. The report suggested that contextualization implies all that is involved in the familiar term indigenization which relates to traditional cultural values, but goes beyond it to take into account very seriously the contemporary factors in cultural change.[126]

According to Ashish Chrispal, contextualization deals with the contemporary socio-economic, political issues of class-caste struggles, power politics, riches and poverty, bribery and corruption, privileges and oppression – all factors that constitute society and the

---

[123] Ashish Chrispal, "Contextualization," in *Doing Mission in Context,* edited by Sunand Sumithra & F. Hrangkhuma (Bangalore: Theological Book Trust, 1995), 1. (Hereafter will be cited as Chrispal, "Contextualization,").

[124] S. Wesley Ariarajha, *Gospel and Culture: An Ongoing Discussion Within the Ecumenical Movement* (Geneva: WCC, 1995), 7.

[125] David J. Bosch, *Transforming Mission: Paradigm Shifts in Theology of Mission* (Maryknoll, NY: Orbis Books, 1991), 448. (Hereafter will be cited as Bosch, *Transforming Mission,*).

[126] Chrispal, "Contextualization," 3. See also Bruce J. Nicholls and Charles H. Kraft, "Anglo-America," in *Contextualization: Meanings, Methods, and Models,* edited by David J. Hesselgrave and Edward Rommen (Grand Rapids, Michigan: Baker Book House, 1989), 48.

relationship between one community and another.[127] David J. Bosch also writes, "Our context comes into play when we interpret a biblical text. One, therefore, has to concede that our theology (or sociology, political theory, etc.) is, by its very nature contextual." For Bosch, one of the emerging paradigms is to see mission as contextualization.[128]

Contextual theologies are claimed, according to Gutierrez, to be theology 'from below,' from the underside of history,' its main source being social sciences, not philosophy as in traditional theology; and its major interlocutor the poor, the oppressed and the exploited, not the educated non – believer as in traditional theology. Thus, it emphasizes priority of praxis and thus theology becomes a critical reflection on Christian praxis in the light of the Word of God.[129]

Darrell L. Whiteman[130] pointed out three functions of contextualization; these three functions may rightly enclose the decisive of contextualization, such as:[131]

i) Contextualization attempts to communicate the Gospel in word and deed and to establish the church in ways that make sense to people within their local cultural context, presenting Christianity in such a way that it meets people's deepest needs and penetrates their worldview, thus allowing them to follow Christ and remain within their own culture.

ii) Another function of contextualization in mission is to offend – but only for the right reasons, not the wrong ones. Good contextualization offends people for the right reasons. Bad

---

[127] Chrispal, "Contextualization," 3.

[128] Bosch, *Transforming Mission,* 423-432.

[129] Gustavo Gutierrez, *A Theology of Liberation: History, Politics and Salvation, translated and edited by Sister Caridad Inda and John Eagleson,* 3rd ed. (Maryknoll, New York: Orbis Books, [1971], 1988), xxix. (Hereafter will be cited as Gutierrez, *A Theology of Liberation,).*

[130] Darrell L. Whiteman is Professor of Cultural Anthropology in the E. Stanley Jones School of World Mission and Evangelization at Asbury Theological Seminary, Wilmore, KY.

[131] Darrell L. Whiteman, "Contextualization: The Theory, the Gap, the Challenge," in *New Directions in Mission & Evangelization 3: Faith and Culture,* edited by James A. Scherer & Stephen B. Bevans (Maryknoll, New York: Orbis Books, 1999), 43-46.

contextualization or the lack of it altogether, offends them for the wrong reasons. When the Gospel is presented in word and deed, and the fellowship of believers we call the church is organized along appropriate cultural patterns, then people will more likely be confronted with the offense of the Gospel, exposing their own sinfulness and the tendency toward evil, oppressive structures and behavior patterns within their culture.

iii) A third function of contextualization in mission is to develop contextualized expressions of the Gospel so that the Gospel itself will be understood in ways the universal church has neither experienced nor understood before, thus expanding our understanding of the kingdom of God. In this sense contextualization is a form of mission in reverse, where we will learn from other cultures how to be more Christian in our own context.

More importantly, theology has to be contextual so that it would meet need of each people instead of universalizing a particular theology for all. As Bultmann sees the Bible as a historical text which needs to be understood in relation to the human existence,[132] we seek the meaningful interpretation and relevant theology for us today.

Liberative

The term liberation theology was first coined in 1968, but received widespread usage in 1973, with the publication of *A Theology of Liberation* by Gustavo Gutierrez, who is known as the father of Liberation theology. His theology is a theology from below, in which the oppressed can speak for themselves. His commitment to mission as liberation is symbolized in his closing words stating that "active participation to human liberation."[133] James Cone emphasized that the main aim of Jesus' salvation is liberation of the oppressed people. He says, "Because human liberation is God's work of salvation in Jesus Christ, its source and meaning cannot be separated from

---

[132] Norman J. Young, *History and Existential Theology: The Role of History in the Thought of Rudolf Bultmann* (Philadelphia: the Westminster Press, 1969), 46.

[133] Norman E. Thomas, *Classic Texts in Mission & World Christianity* (Maryknoll, New York: Orbis Books, 1995), 185. (Hereafter will be cited as Thomas, *Classic Texts in mission,*).

Christological sources (Scripture, tradition, and social existence) and content (Jesus in his past, present, and future)." Cone strongly opined that Christ's salvation is liberation; there is no liberation without Christ. Both meanings are inherent in the statement that Jesus Christ is the ground of human liberation.[134]

Liberation theology is a radical new approach for the theological task that begins with the poor, especially the poor classes of the third world, and recognizes God's presence in their struggle to throw off oppression.[135] According to Cone, Christian Theology is language about God's liberating activity in the world on behalf of the freedom of the oppressed. Any talk about God that fails to make God's liberation of the oppressed its starting points is not Christian.[136] The scopes of liberation theology are Latin American liberation theology, Black theology, Feminist theology, Dalit/Tribal theology and other contextual theologies.

Theological implications of Liberation theology:

1) *Biblical approach:* Jurgen Moltmann, a famous theologian says, "Reading the Bible with the eyes of the poor is a different thing from reading it with the eyes of man [sic] with a full belly."[137] The biblical approach of the liberation theologian is rightly from the perspective of the poor and marginalized people. They interpret the Bible and doctrine of the church from the eyes of the needy persons. Especially the Exodus event is the prototype for God's liberation movement. They taught that the Old Testament prophets were the protesters of injustice, indicator of social reality and the

---

[134] James Hal Cone, *God of the Oppressed* (New York: HarperCollin Publishers, 1975), 141. (Hereafter will be cited as Cone, *God of the Oppressed,*).

[135] Stanley J. Grenz & Roger E. Olson, *20th Century Theology: God & the World in a Transitional Age* (Secunderabad: OM Books, 2004), 211. (Hereafter will be cited as Stanley J. Grenz & Roger E. Olson, *20th Century Theology,*).

[136] James H. Cone, *Speaking The Truth: Ecumenism, Liberation, and Black Theology* (Grand Rapids, Michigan: William B. Eermans Publishing Company, 1986), 4.

[137] Jurgen Moltmann, *The Church in the power of Spirit* (London: SCM Press, 1977), 17.

conscientizers.[138] The Biblical bases of liberation theology are mostly base on the two passages of both the Old Testament and the New Testament, such as Exod 3:7-8 and Luke 4:18-19 respectively.[139] From the Feminist perspective, the traditional biblical approach is largely responsible for the subordination of women. It seems that the traditional biblical hermeneutics did not give liberative in their status. So, they have been creatively reconstructing Christian theology with feminist questions in mind. They point out not only the absence of women in history, but they try to recover the lost histories of women, developing a new theological methodology, inventing a new hermeneutics, reformulating a new ecclesiology and Christology and reconstructing the doctrine of human and God.[140]

2) *Sin:* According to Gutiérrez, the biblical language of sin and salvation became closely identified with the Marxist notion of class warfare. In Liberation Theology, sin is not considered as an individual, private, or merely interior reality. Sin is regarded as a social, historical fact, the absence of brother/sisterhood and love in relationships among human.[141] So also, salvation is not understood as a souls being rescued for heaven, but as the process of liberation from oppression and injustice. Jesus is a social liberator par excellence.

---

[138] B. Zirsangliana, *Theology Kalphung Hrang Hrangte* (Aizawl: Lalremsiami, 2011), 132-133. (Hereafter will be cited as Zirsangliana, *Theology Kalphung,*).

[139] "Then the LORD said, 'I have observed the misery of my people who are in Egypt, I have heard their cry on account of their taskmasters. Indeed, I know their sufferings, and I have come down to deliver them from the Egyptians, and to bring them up out of that land to a good and broad land, a land flowing with milk and honey…'"(Exod 3:7-8)."The spirit of the Lord is upon me, because he has anointed me to bring good news to the poor. He has sent me to proclaim release to the captives and recovery of sight to the blind, to let the oppressed go free, to proclaim the year of the Lord's favour" (Luke 4:18-19).

[140] K. Thanzauva, "Theological Education for Social Transformation: A Feminist Perspective," in *Transforming Theology for Empowering Women: A Theological Hermeneutical Reflection In The Context of North East India,* edited by R. L. Hnuni (Jorhat: ETC, Women Studies, 1999), 91. (Hereafter will be cited as Thanzauva, "Theological Education for Social Transformation:,).

[141] Gustavo Gutierrez, *A Theology of Liberation*, 85.

3) *God:* Liberation theologians criticize the traditional theology of God which stress transcendental God. But, liberation theology emphasizes the immanence of God saying 'God is Immanent God' who is always involving in human activities. One good example is the Black theology that emphasized the immanence of God, the pioneer James Cone described as "God always encounters us in a situation of historical liberation."[142]

4) *Jesus Christ:* Traditional theology plainly emphasize that Jesus' salvific work is salvation from sin and saving soul, but Liberation theology emphasizes on the socio-economic and political liberation aspect of the people.[143] The hermeneutical principle for an exegesis of the Scriptures is the revelation of God in Christ as the Liberator of the oppressed from social oppression and to political struggle, wherein the poor recognize that their fight against poverty and injustice is not only consistent with the gospel but is the gospel of Jesus Christ.[144] For tribal liberation, Mawrie asserts, "The Tribal people in India are a "no people" who exist at the periphery of society. Like the Hebrews who were a "no people" before their liberation from Egypt but became a chosen people of God, so too Christ must be presented as a Saviour who restores to them their dignity and identity"[145]

5) *Church:* Liberation theology emphasizes the purpose of the church rather than what the church is. The fifth WCC Assembly in Nairobi 1975 judged the goals of UN's decade for development in the 1960s as inadequate and called upon the churches "to share

---

[142] James H. Cone, *A Black Theology of Liberation* (Maryknoll, New York: Orbis Books, 1986), 141. (Hereafter will be cited as Cone, *A Black Theology of Liberation*).

[143] Ahao Vashum, "Emerging Vision of Indigenous/Tribal Theology," in *Dalit-Tribal Theological Interface: Current Trends in Subaltern Theologies*, edited by James Massey & Shimreingam Shimray (Jorhat & New Delhi: TSC/WSC & CDS, 2007), 25.

[144] James H. Cone, *God of the Oppressed* (New York: HarperCollins Publishers, 1975), 81-82. (Hereafter will be cited as Cone, *God of the Oppressed,*).

[145] Barnes L. Mawrie, "Experience of the Tribal Historical, Political, Socio-Cultural Contexts: Quest for a Tribal Theology," in *Dalit-Tribal Theological Interface: Current Trends in Subaltern Theologies*, edited by James Massey & Shimreingam Shimray (Jorhat & New Delhi: TSC/WSC & CDS, 2007), 94.

with the oppressed their struggle for liberation." The Third World theologians embraced the new paradigm in the EATWOT conference of 1976, calling upon theologians to be committed "to a lifestyle of solidarity with the poor and the oppressed and involvement in their action with them." Following Christ the liberator, Christian churches are called to join the struggle against all oppression and exploitation.[146] It is the liberation from sin in all its manifestations of alienation from God and neighbor. It is liberation from economic exploitation, dehumanization, and oppression. It is liberation from meaninglessness and self-alienation, from poverty and suffering. It is liberation toward a meaningful human existence seeking freedom and human fulfillment, liberation for the service of the living God. For the churches this liberation involves joining the struggle against political oppression and economic exploitation; against racism and all forms of degradation; against the destruction of human beingness wherever it may occur on the continent.[147]

5) *Salvation:* According to liberation theology, salvation is not something otherworldly, in regard to which the present life is merely a test. Salvation is something which embraces all human reality, transforms it, and leads it to its fullness in Christ.[148] The Reign of God that Jesus preached expresses human's Utopia[149] longing

---

[146] Thomas, *Classic Texts in mission*, 185.

[147] Thomas, *Classic Texts in mission*, 196.

[148] Gutierrez, *A Theology of Liberation*, 85.

[149] The term *utopia* (from the Greek *ou-topos*, "no place," or *eu-topos*, "good place," and evidently coined as a pun by Thomas More for the title of his book published in 1516) has very diverse, often confusing connotations. Sometimes it is used to mean any idealization of the distant or primordial past, when humans lived closer to the gods (or God), as found in Sumero-Akkadian cuneiform accounts of Dilman; in the Hebrew story of Eden of Genesis; in portrayals of the Golden Age by Hesiod, Vergil, Symmachus, and other Greek and Roman writers; in myths of the "perfect great period' in later Vedic, earlier Jain, and Buddhist traditions; or in accounts of the early age of the four (mythic) emperors of popular Chinese thought. In contrast, the term utopia at other times refers to the future realization of some perfect place and time. It can take on futurist instead of primitivist associations, thus becoming a lost paradise regained, the projection of the hopes and dreams of a millenarianism, or establishment of an ideal society divinely or otherwise sanctioned to replace the glaring ills of the day. A more traditional understanding of

for liberation from everything that alienates him, factors such as anguish, pain, hunger, injustice, oppression and slavery. Salvation is something that effects all creation and all inter-human relations, autonomous, interpersonal, and social. Since the reign enters a sin-permeated world, a world of oppression and exploitation, salvation is to be understood as an all embracing liberation, that is, in a holistic sense.[150] Gutierrez opined that liberation and salvation is similar and equal terms. He mentioned the dimensions of liberation in Christ as: 1) there is liberation from oppressive socio-economic structures to live in conditions contrary to God's will for their life, 2) personal transformation by which we live with profound inner freedom in the face of every kind of servitude, 3) liberation from sin, which attacks the deepest root of all servitude.[151]

Theological emphasis of Liberation Theology: Gutierrez rightly asserts, "Liberation theology is a critical reflection on Christian praxis in the light of the word of God."[152] This is a theological method of Liberation theology. To liberation theologians, theology is not only a timeless truth but it should be changed according to various servitudes. There is theological emphasis of liberation theology; we will look at as under:

1) *The preferential option for the poor:* One of the central themes of liberation theology is that all theology and mission arises out of the preferential option for the poor. In the present revolutionary situation characterized by class struggle and conflict, the church must cast its lot with the oppressed, because in history God-self is on the side of the poor.[153] Gutierrez explained: "the poor deserve preference not because they are morally or religiously better than others, but because God is God, in whose eyes 'the last are first.' This

---

utopia (as in Thomas More) is that of a distant, wondrous land allegedly discovered and described by a traveller returning home. Garry W. Trompf, "Utopia" in *The Encyclopaedia of Religion Volume 15 Trad – Zwin*, edited by Mircea Eliade et al. (New York: Macmillan Publishing Company, 1987), 159-162.

[150] William Jenkinson & Helen O'Sullivan, *Trends in Mission: Toward the Third Millennium* (Maryknoll, New York: Orbis Books, 1993), 75.

[151] Gutierrez, *A Theology of Liberation,* xxxviii.

[152] Gutierrez, *A Theology of Liberation,* xxix.

[153] Stanley J. Grenz & Roger E. Olson, *20th Century Theology,* 218.

statement clashes with our narrow understanding of justice; this very preference reminds us, therefore, that God's ways are not ours."[154]

2) *Institutional Violence:* Liberation theologians opined that the institution of government administrative structure has already oppressed the poor and the elite groups always dominate the proletariat people. The church also has been neglecting that the rich dominates the poor, which is lucidly wrong.[155] Therefore, for Gutierrez, poverty is a situation that destroys peoples, families, and individuals; that is called "Institutionalized violence."[156]

3) *Structural sin:* Structural analysis has played an important part in building up the picture of the world to which liberation theology address itself. As far as poverty is concerned, an important transformation is undoubtedly taking place in the social analysis on which liberation theology depends to some extent.[157] Liberation theologians emphasize that human beings need to be saved from structural sin rather than individual sin. And that saving from structural sin will transform the individual life and all aspects of human situations.

4) *Orthopraxis:* Orthopraxis simply means correct action. The praxis on which liberation theology reflects is praxis of solidarity in the interests of liberation and is inspired by the gospel. It is the activity of "peacemakers" – that is, those who are forging shalom. This liberating praxis endeavors to transform history in the light of the reign of God.[158] Liberation theology is an attempt to discern the

---

[154] Gutierrez, *A Theology of Liberation…, xxxviii.* According to Gutierrez, the term "option" has not always been correctly understood. Like every term, it has its limitations; the intention in using it is to emphasize the freedom and commitment expressed in a decision. The commitment to the poor is not "optional" in the sense that a Christian is free to make or not make this option, or commitment, to the poor, just as the love owe to all human beings without exception is not "optional." Neither, on the other hand, does the world of the poor. In very many instances, of course, they do not, but it must be said at the same time that the poor too have an obligation to make this option. Gutierrez, *A Theology of Liberation…*, xxvi.

[155] Zirsangliana, *Theology Kalphung,* 138.

[156] Gutierrez, *A Theology of Liberation,* xxi.

[157] Gutierrez, *A Theology of Liberation*, xxiv.

[158] Gutierrez, *A Theology of Liberation,* xxx.

action of God in history and to collaborate with it by transforming the world. It starts with the experience of poverty, misery, oppression, and a new awareness that such human situations can be changed by the analysis and exposure of their root causes and consequently their elimination.[159]

Liberation theology emphasized that Jesus is not only soul's Saviour but the Saviour of the oppressed and marginalized people. Since they stressed that saving from oppression and to build up justice, equality and dignity for the downtrodden people, liberation theology is different from other theological disciplines, so it is called 'Christian Socialism.'[160] Mary Daly, a feminist theologian says, "Real liberation is not merely unrestricted genital activity ("the sexual revolution"), but free and defiant thinking, willing, imaging, speaking, creating, acting. It is be-ing.[161] The liberation of language is rooted in the liberation of ourselves."[162] Cone rightly defines theology as the discipline that seeks to analyze the nature of Christian in the light of the oppressed arises chiefly from biblical tradition itself.[163] From the eyes of feminist theology, re-reading the Bible and re-construct traditional theology is one of the liberation theologies. For them, the aim of a re-reading is to un-cover women's absences as well as to discover women's presences throughout the history of the Christian church and in those texts the Christian church considers relevant and normative.[164] Thus, feminist theologians are engaged themselves in the task of liberating traditional theology from male bias and male chauvinism. In the attempt to transform the traditional theology, feminist theologians take as their first agenda the criticism of masculine bias of Christian theology. This bias has excluded women from ordained

---

[159] Kuncheria Pathil & Dominic Veliath, eds. *An Introduction to Theology* (Bangalore: Theological Publications of India, 2005), 217-218.

[160] Zirsangliana, *Theology Kalphung,* 141.

[161] Mary Daly, *Beyond God the Father: Toward a Philosophy of Women* (Boston: Beacon Press, 1973), 179. (Hereafter will be cited as Daly, *Beyond God the Father,*).

[162] Daly, *Beyond God the Father,* 8.

[163] Cone, *A Black Theology of Liberation*, 2.

[164] Natalie K. Watson, *Feminist Theology* (Grand Rapids, Michigan: William B. Eerdmans Publishing Company, 2003), 5.

ministry, decision making bodies other important responsibilities and leadership.[165] As Cone expressed that Jesus is the ground of our present freedom to struggle and the source of our hope… In this sense, liberation is not a human possession but a divine gift of freedom to those who struggle in faith against violence and oppression.[166]

Transformation

Biblical hermeneutics for social transformation is a kind of liberation theology. It is very popular among the Indian Christian theologians. These changes always reflect the life of the people. In his book *Hindu Response to the Unbound Christ,* Samartha says that Christ is always involved in human situations, wherever the struggle for justice, freedom and truth is going on, and demands that his followers also participate in his crucifixion and resurrection. And he cannot be bound or identified with any particular cultural situation nor to a particular system and thought.[167] M. M. Thomas also emphasized the inclusive nature of salvation saying:

> Salvation includes community and unity among humankind. God has raised Jesus from among the dead as the guarantee of the final victory of God and human over all evil in individuals, society and the cosmos, and over death. Through God's spirit God has brought into being the Church, the community of those who believe in Christ to be a witness to the renewal of all things in Christ; to co-operate with God in it and to be a foretaste of it in its life. In the End, God will transform the Kingdoms [sic] of this world into the Kingdom [sic] of God and His [sic] Christ.[168]

---

[165] Thanzauva, "Theological Education for Social Transformation:, 91.

[166] Cone, *God of the Oppressed,* 138.

[167] Cited by Sunand Sumithra, *Christian Theologies From an Indian Perspective* (Bangalore: Theological Book Trust, 1995), 195.

[168] M. M. Thomas, "The Secular Ideologies of India and the Secular Meaning of Christ," in *Readings in Indian Christian Theology -1,* edited by R. S. Sugirtharajah & Cecil Hargreaves (Delhi: ISPCK, 1993), 96.

Social transformation is beginning from the realization of the Reign of God here and now and it is the goal of today's theology. Jesus taught that God's reign is in our midst (Lk. 18:21). This is a constructive element of proclaiming the gospel since the ultimate goal of the Reign is the transformation of the whole of creation. K. Thanzauva argues that in concrete terms, this realization of the Reign of God here and now means building a just, free, participatory, progressive, harmonious and sustainable society.[169] Bosch also observed that Luke concept of salvation includes the total transformation of human life, forgiveness of sin, healing from infirmities, and release from any kind of bondage.[170] According to Gutierrez, the centre of God's salvific design is Jesus Christ, who by his death and resurrection transforms the universe and makes it possible for the person to reach fulfillment as a human being. This fulfillment embraces every aspect of humanity: body and spirit, individual and society, person and cosmos, time and eternity. Christ, the image of God the (Father) and the perfect God-Man, takes on all the dimensions of human existence.[171]

The Nazareth periscope is the basis of Luke's entire gospel and today's transformation theology. In Luke, proclamation of the gospel is explained with two very modern sounding qualifications: First, a strong emphasis is placed upon the gospel's address to the poor. The gospel is for the poor. Secondly, proclamation in word is closely linked with concrete deeds of liberation breaking through the structures of oppression and injustice that force the poor into their situation of poverty and hold them there by violence. Mission thus aims to restructure society as a whole on a global scale.[172]

When we look at the salvific work of Jesus, Christ has connected his liberation with the struggles of the miserable life of the earth. Many Christians seldom understand that Jesus' salvation

---

[169] Thanzauva, *Theology of Community,* 54.

[170] Bosch, *Transforming Mission,* 107.

[171] Gutierrez, *A Theology of Liberation,* 85.

[172] M. R. Spindler, "The Biblical Grounding and Orientation of Mission," in *Missiology: An Ecumenical Introduction* F. J. Verstraelen et al. (Grand Rapids, Michigan: William B. Eerdmans Publishing Company, 1995), 130.

is horizontal including socio-eco-political and religion but their understanding is limited only to a vertical ideology like, longing for departure from this miserable earthly life and to live in the place of all pleasures called heaven. But, the salvific work of Christ would be meaningless without touching the mundane reality of the life of the concerned persons.

Social Gospel

In the 19th century, American people emphasized the individual life and rights. In their spiritual life they also emphasized individual salvation. The Social Gospel movement is a Protestant Christian intellectual movement that was most prominent in the early 20th century United States and Canada. The Social Gospel affected much of Protestant America. The Presbyterians described its goals in 1910 by proclaiming:[173] The movement applied Christian ethics to social problems, especially issues of social justice such as excessive wealth, poverty, liquor, crime, racial tensions, slums, bad hygiene, child labour, inadequate labour unions, poor schools, and the danger of war.[174]

Theories regarding the decline of the Social Gospel after World War I often cite the rise of neo-orthodoxy as a contributing factor in the movement's decline. Some believe that many of the Social Gospel's ideas reappeared in the Civil Rights Movement of the 1960s. "Social Gospel" principles continue to inspire newer movements such as Christians Against Poverty.[175] The great ends of the church are the proclamation of the gospel for the salvation of humankind; the shelter, nurture, and spiritual fellowship of the children of God; the maintenance of divine worship; the preservation of truth; the promotion of social righteousness; and the exhibition of the Reign of Heaven to the world.[176]

---

[173] *Social Gospel,* http://en.wikipedia.org/wiki/Social_Gospel (24.11.2011).

[174] *Social Gospel,* http://en.wikipedia.org/wiki/Social_Gospel (24.11.2011).

[175] *Social Gospel,* http://en.wikipedia.org/wiki/Social_Gospel (24.11.2011).

[176] "Social Gospel," http://en.wikipedia.org/wiki/Social_Gospel (24 Nov. 2011).

In the late 19th century, many Americans were disgusted by the poverty level and the low quality of living in the slums. The social gospel movement provided a religious rationale for action to address those concerns. Activists in the Social Gospel movement hoped that by public health measures as well as enforced schooling so the poor could develop talents and skills, the quality of their moral lives would begin to improve. In a Theology for the Social Gospel, Rauschenbusch[177] states that the individualistic gospel has made sinfulness of the individual clear, but it has not shed light on institutionalized sinfulness: "It has not evoked faith in the will and power of God to redeem the permanent institutions of human society from their inherited guilt of oppression and extortion."[178] This ideology would be inherited by liberation theologians and civil rights advocates and leaders such as Martin Luther King Jr.[179]

---

[177] The Most important exponent of the Social Gospel was Walter Rauschenbusch (1861-1918), a German-American Baptist who ministered for ten years in New York City's 'Hell's Kitchen' before becoming a professor of church History at Rochester Seminary in the state of New York. Rauschenbusch's firsthand experience of industrial exploitation and governmental indifference to workers made him a convinced critic of the established order. His fruitful relationships with New York City socialists like Henry George (1839-97) offered alternative models for social organization. But Rauschenbusch's main concern was to search the Scriptures for a message to the troubled circumstances of industrial society. The results of this search were published in 1907 as *Christianity and the Social Crisis*, a work that recalled the prophetic denunciations of Old Testament prophets of mammon. Rauschenbusch followed this work with other influential volumes, including *Prayers of the Social Awakening* (1912), *Christianizing the Social Order* (1912), and *A Theology for the Social Gospel* (1917). In these works Rauschenbusch combined the Kingdom of God through the power of Christ. [M.A. Noll, "Social Gospel," *New Dictionary of Theology*, edited by Sinclair B. Ferguson, et al., 1988, Reprint (Leicester, England: InterVarsity Press, 2005), 646-647]. (Hereafter will be cited as Noll, "Social Gospel,").

[178] Walter Rauschenbusch, *A Theology for the Social Gospel* (New York: Abingdon Press, 1917), 5. (Henceforth will be cited as Rauschenbusch, *A Theology for the Social Gospel,*).

[179] "Social Gospel," http://en.wikipedia.org/wiki/Social_Gospel (24 Nov. 2011).

The Social Gospel is often identified with theological liberalism, and with some justice. Washington Gladden,[180] for example, was an individual who popularized of biblical higher criticism, and Walter Rauschenbusch, though much more realistic about the intractably fallen character of human nature, yet reinterpreted some traditionally supernatural elements of Christian doctrine. At the same time, however, themes of social service association with the Social Gospel were also prominent among evangelical bodies such as the Salvation Army or in individual evangelical leaders like A. J. Gordon (1836-1895) in Boston. Since the 1930s the Social Gospel has disappeared as a movement in its own right, but its influence remains, both in the more liberal, mainline denominations and in the renewed social concern displayed by American Evangelicals since 1960s.[181]

Theological Implications of the Social Gospel:

1) *Collective Salvation:* The main message of social Gospel theology is collective salvation rather than individual salvation which was emphasized by Evangelical Theology. It emphasized that not only individual souls but entire corporate entities and social structures would repent and be saved.[182] Its origins link in the American revival tradition between personal holiness and social reform contributed to the movement; as did as also the newer concern for scientific study of social problems that accompanied

---

[180] Early expression of the Social Gospel included the work of Washington Gladden (1836-1918), a Congregationalist minister in Springfield, Massachusetts he had published *Working People and Their Employers* (1876), an appeal for fairness to workers. In his Ohio congregation were mine owners whose labourers struck twice in the mid-1880s for better wages and working conditions. Gladden's belief in the justice of their demands led to a more insistent appeal for the rights of labour and the application of the 'Golden Rule' to industrial organization. A different expression of the Social Gospel appeared in the work of Charles Sheldon (1857-1946), a clergyman from Topeka, Kansas, whose best-selling novel *In His Steps* (1897) presented a picture of what could happen in a community torn by social dissension if Christians would only ask themselves in every decision, 'What would Jesus Do?' Noll, "Social Gospel," 646-647.

[181] Noll, "Social Gospel," 646-647.

[182] Stanley J. Grenz & Roger E. Olson, *20th Century Theology,* 61.

the rise of modern America after the Civil War.[183] According to Walter Rauschenbusch, the essential Christian task is not so much to abolish drunkenness and adultery, but "to transform human society into the Reign of God by regenerating all human relations and reconciling them in accordance with the will of God."[184] Important concerns of the Social Gospel movement were labor reforms, such as abolishing child labor and regulating the hours of work by mothers. By 1920 they were crusading against the 12-hour day for workers at U.S. Steel.[185]

2) *The Reign of God here on earth:* Likewise liberation theology, the "Reign of God" is crucial to Rauschenbusch's proposed theology of the social gospel. He states that the ideology and doctrine of the "the Reign of God," of which Jesus Christ reportedly "always spoke"[186] has been gradually replaced by that of the Church. This was done at first by the early church out of what appeared to be necessity, but Rauschenbusch calls Christians to return to the doctrine of "the Reign of God."[187] Of course, such a replacement has cost theology and Christians at large a great deal: the way we view Jesus and the synoptic gospels, the ethical principles of Jesus, and worship rituals have all been affected by this replacement.[188] In promoting a return to the doctrine of the "Reign of God," he clarified that the "Reign of God": is not subject to the pitfalls of the Church; it can test and correct the Church; is a prophetic, future-focused ideology and a revolutionary, social and political force that understands all creation to be sacred; and it can help save the problematic, sinful social order.[189]

---

[183] Noll, "Social Gospel," 646-647.

[184] Walter Rauschenbusch, *Christianity and the Social Crisis* (New York: Macmillan, 1907), xi, cited by Stanley J. Grenz & Roger E. Olson, *20th Century Theology,* 61.

[185] "Social Gospel," http://en.wikipedia.org/wiki/Social_Gospel (24 Nov. 2011).

[186] Rauschenbusch, *A Theology for the Social Gospel,* 131.

[187] Rauschenbusch, *A Theology for the Social Gospel,* 132.

[188] Rauschenbusch, *A Theology for the Social Gospel,* 132.

[189] Rauschenbusch, *A Theology for the Social Gospel,* 134-137.

Social Gospel theologians did not explicitly deny the classical doctrine of the Christian faith, but especially, Rauschenbusch reinterpreted them in the light of the central unifying theme of the Reign of God.[190] Theologically, the Social Gospellers sought to operationalize the Lord's Prayer (Matthew 6:10): "Your kingdom come, your will be done, on earth as it is in heaven" (Mat. 6:10).[191] They emphasized that the reality of Reign of God in the midst of the people. As Jesus proclaimed the Reign, he positively involved in every spheres of life, spiritual, social, economic and ecological. This can rule out any doubt about the range of the gospel of God's Reign. The good news of the Reign of God provoked the hearers to go beyond the nationalistic boundaries to which they restricted it. When we see mission in the light of the Reign, we are challenged to break out from the narrow confinement we have set for God's reign.[192] As Lesslie Newbigin said that the Reign of God is not one sector of human affairs, but it is over all things.[193] The Reign of God is an inclusive society where widows, orphans, aliens, and down trodden were full members. The Reign of God proved to be a theological and ideological weapon for the oppressed. This concept as taught by Jesus was a critique of the powers and the principalities, accordingly the Reign of God would protect the weak and the powerless (Deut 10:17, 18).[194]

Conclusion

When we look at the above selected reading paradigms, It is plainly emphasized that the concept of Reign of God *here and now* or *realized eschatology* was inaugurated coming of Jesus and his ministry. It is trying to make use the redemptive reign of God

---

[190] Stanley J. Grenz & Roger E. Olson, *20th Century Theology:*, 61.

[191] "Social Gospel," http://en.wikipedia.org/wiki/Social_Gospel (24 Nov. 2011).

[192] Ken Gnanakan, *Kingdom Concerns A Theology of Mission Today* (Leicester: IVP, 1989), 113-114. (Hereafter will be cited as Gnanakan, *Kingdom Concerns,*).

[193] Gnanakan, *Kingdom Concerns*, 115.

[194] Moses P. Manohar, "Kingdom of God the Test of the Church," in *Church Towards Understanding Mission and Witness,* Edt. By Moses P. Manohar (Chennai: ICSA/ISPCK, 2002), 23.

energetically by the active to establish God's rule among human in socio-economic, political and religious dimension. The theology from 'below' is the central message of above points and it tells us to know that service to God means service to humankind. And it is clearly indicated that unless our biblical hermeneutics give us libeartive and transformative in all spheres of our life, Bible would be meaningless and it does not convey Good News for humankinds. So, biblical hermeneutics would be significant, hopeful and relevant for the concern persons.

Chapter 4

A Theological Appraisal of Zairema's Understanding of the Bible from the Selected Reading Paradigms

Introduction

It may not be fair to study Zairema's biblical approach in isolation from other aspects of his thought. Since it is assumed that the various aspects of Zairema's thought are integrally related, one cannot avoid having at least a general survey of some of the selected paradigms of Zairema's theology. In this chapter we will analyse the main trust of Zairema's approach to the Bible and evaluate his approach in order to provide a theoretical framework for social and moral reformation among the Mizo.

A Critique of Zairema's Approach to the Bible from the Selected Hermeneutical Paradigms

K. Thanzauva, one of the Mizo Systematic theologians says that tribal Christians are mostly Biblicists who try to use the Bible as a magical book to provide ready-made answers to solve their problems.[195] Zairema also opined that Mizo Christians are quite Biblicist and many people consider the Bible as a magical book. Most people never seem to consider that it is the book of God's intervention and the history of salvation of humankind. Therefore, as Lasetso argued, the method of traditional reading practiced among the tribal Christians is not liberative,[196] and because of this, Zairema strongly asserted that the conventional way of teaching of the Bible as well as the traditional teaching needs re-looking and re-consideration in order to draw out its liberative nature.[197] Though the centrality of scripture as a formative factor of Zairema's theology is undisputed, yet it must be noted that Zairema's theological method with its central emphasis upon the authority of the Bible is radically different from most of the evangelical groups of his Church and lay theologians among the Mizo. While emphasizing the primacy of the scripture, Zairema does not neglect other important factors in doing theology. He attaches much importance in his theological methodology to the ecclesial tradition and highly values healthy Christian tradition. He makes good use of the tradition in his theological implication. His theological methodology can be termed as liberative, contextual and biblical. At the same time, as we already mentioned in the previous chapter he found 'Historical Critical Method' to be very useful for implementing his biblical hermeneutics. His theological methodology and method of biblical hermeneutics lucidly appeared in his biblical approach and theological implications.

It is vividly visible that Zairema made used of socio-scientific criticism for his biblical approach. Socio-scientific criticism is an attempt to reconstruct the social worlds behind the biblical texts, and at the same time giving light to the lives of people living in these

---

[195] Thanzauva, *Theology of Community*, 91.

[196] Razouselie Lasetso, "The Word of God and the Tribal Response," in *Dalit-Tribal Theological Interface: Current Trends in Subaltern Theologies*, edited by James Massey & Shimreigam Shimray (ETC Jorhat & New Delhi: TSC/WSC & CDS, 2007), 176.

[197] Zairema, *Kan Bible Hi*, 241.

worlds.[198] We will analyze his approach to the Bible from the selected hermeneutical paradigms as the followings:

Contextual

Zairema was very much concerned with contextual hermeneutical approach of the Bible; he says that for the (Mizo) theologians to express God's revelation in terms and language which are natural to Mizos "we need not listen with English ears."[199] He was very much concerned with dynamic equivalent translation in translating the Bible which becomes a guideline for BSI. He made use of this instruction in his theological articulations. He urged that Mizoram theological students must seek relevancy for exposition of salvation.

---

[198] Sociological interpretation or socio-scientific criticism is part of the wider enterprise of historical criticism of the Bible. Sociological interpretation attends to questions of a different but related kind. These are concerned with the typical social patterns and taken-for-granted cultural conceptions most likely to have characterized the biblical world and influenced the biblical writers. {N. Steinberg, "Social Scientific Criticism," in *Dictionary of Biblical Interpretation, k – z,* edited by John H. Hayes, et al. (Nashville: Abingdon Press, 1999), 478}. Robert Mulholland cites five levels that operate interactively in the use of Sociological Criticism in the NT: - **1**. The preliminary level, which is mostly descriptive. It studies the social setting from textual, archeological and inscriptional evidences. **2**. A more analytical description of the social dynamics, understanding the interactions between various social structures in NT society. **3.** The analysis and description of how different social groups and individuals exist and function within the sociological matrix of their world. **4.** With insights from the study of the sociological matrix, the text of the NT is studied. The meaning of the words and symbols of the text are sought within the context of this social matrix, not that of the interpreter. **5.** As hinted above, a careful distinction must be maintained between the sociological horizon of the interpreter and that of the text. The interpreter tries to enter the world of the text and its community of faith and to draw out the meaning of the text within that life-matrix. Only after this can transfer of meaning be made and analogues be located in the interpreter's own social matrix. {M. Robert Mulholland Jr., "Sociological Criticism," in *New Testament Criticism and Interpretation,* edited by David Alan Black and David S. Dockery (Grand Rapids, Michigan: Zondervan Publishing House, 1991), 303-304.}.

[199] Zairema, "A Quest for Indigenous Expression of Christianity in Mizoram," *Ground Works for Tribal Theology in the Mizo Context,* edited by Rosiamliana Tochhawng et al. (Delhi: ISPCK, 2007), 124. (Hereafter will be cited as Zairema, "A Quest for Indigenous Expression,).

He says that individual salvation of the soul is understandable, but the thought that salvation from Hell to Heaven shall take place at some distant future has little relevance to our daily problem. Our preaching of salvation of God has to be relevant to make it effective in our lives.[200] We may say that Zairema adapted to some extent contextualization as his method of doing theology. So, far as his theological methodology is concerned, Zairema is not far behind and contemporary theology can benefit from it. Meanwhile, as this study focuses on an attempt to identify which aspects of Zairema's theology are significant for the Mizo Christians and which are not, it can be said that contextualization is not relevant enough among the churchgoer who are bounded by traditional mindset. It seems that contextualization is limited inside the church, and cannot be relevant enough because some contextual theologies used to reject the church traditional practices and rituals of the worship. Some contextual theologians like Tribal theologians have been 'romanticizing' the tribal world view in an attempt to rediscover liberative motifs in tribal culture and become 'eclectic' (a tendency to be selective from the Gospel and culture), which would hardly be successful. Rosiamliana Tochhawng says that these are quite dangerous for rediscovering tribal heritage.[201] Therefore, one has to be careful in introducing among the churchgoer. If one make use of it for rejecting some traditional theology it cannot be too

---

[200] Zairema, *Random Notes*, 18.

[201] Rosiamliana Tochhawng, "Methodological Reflection on Theologizing Tribal Heritage in North East India," *Theologizing Tribal Heritage: A Critical Re-Look,* edited by Hrangthan Chhungi (Delhi: CWM, ISET-ECC, PCI, ISPCK, 2008), 26-27. Rosiamliana says that there is a danger of becoming 'eclectic'; a tendency to be selective from the Gospel and culture, which would hardly be successful. There would be a tendency to employ only those cultural elements, which were manifestedly neutral and naturally good, failing thus to understand the configuration of culture that one or more elements of a culture cannot really be disassembled without disturbing the culture whole. The second danger is 'romanticizing' the tribal world view in an attempt to rediscover liberative motifs in tribal culture.

credible enough. In his Biblical approach, it can be seen that Zairema's contextualization. We will enumerate as under:

1) Bible is the Book of God's Revelation and the Book of Salvation History: It is plainly visible that the Bible is the book of God's revelation in Zairema's biblical approach. He opined that the Bible is the book of God's revelation which is written by the receivers of God's word and wrote as best as they could for others. To him, Jesus Christ is the final revelation of God. Although, NT is the narration of Jesus, all the books of NT are not the perfect revelation of God. Even though the authors of the Bible saw the perfect revelation, but they could not know it completely.[202] For Zairema, while they wanted to understand the meaning of the messages, the authors of the Bible incorporated several of their ideas, and they choose relevant terms for their readers. It seems that they used the common language which was not complicated for the ordinary people in those times while writing the Bible. Owing to the fact that languages of the Bible are very ancient and complicated to grasp for the modern ears, we need scholars to explain the meanings for contemporary world. Zairema argued that the main reason of God's revelation is to have mutual fellowship with human beings.[203]

Zairema and Karl Barth's understanding of revelation is closely related. According to Karl Barth, revelation, however, finds expression in the Bible as witness to God's revelation, and it is a witness to "the lordship of the triune God." In the Bible we encounter "human words written in human speech," which witness to revelation.[204] Thus, the central theme of Barth's teaching on revelation is a biblical one that revelation is none other than God revealing Godself in Jesus Christ. According to him, it seems that the revelation is not something separate from God. It is God's Godself in action.[205] So, he maintains that human beings cannot know God apart from Jesus Christ. It

---

[202] Zairema, *Kan Bible HI,* 234.

[203] Zairema, *Kan Bible Hi*, 273.

[204] Karl Barth, *Church Dogmatics* I/2 (Edinburg: T&T Clark, 1956), 458, 463, cited by Antony Thiselton, *Hermeneutics: An Introduction* (Grand Rapids, Michigan: William B. Eerdmans Publishing Company, 2009), 188.

[205] Colin Brown, *Karl Barth and the Christian Message* (London: Tyndale Press, 1977), 144.

seems that human beings cannot know by their own ability or by general revelation in creation and history.[206] According to Barth, "the Bible is God's Word so far as God lets it be his [sic] Word"[207] These are not similar with the acceptance of some conservative among the Protestant Churches. On the other hand, it seems that Zairema never thought God as transcendental like the Neo-Orthodox theologians, but is an Immanent God. Like many liberal theologians, Zairema applied critical methods to show that the Bible is not historically accurate. Zairema strongly holds that the Bible is the book of spiritual salvation history and it is the book that indicates God's plans for human being to return to the right status.[208] Many liberal theologians opined that the authors were primarily theologians and not historians, so the "Jesus of history" is nothing like the Jesus of the Bible. This means that if there is a discrepancy between the Bible and other historical material, it is the Bible that is most probably in error. A Biblical account must be 'proved' historically accurate rather than accepted as so.[209] It seems that Zairema was also concerned with the business of the authors whose interest were in God's salvation history rather than historically accuracy. He tries to disclose the main aim of the Bible through his definition of revelation, though it seems that his approach to the Bible is dissimilar from Evangelical perspective, yet when we critically analyse it, his understanding is more relevant and has lasting impact for Mizo Christians.

2) Emphasizing God's Message Rather Than Miracles: Zairema's approach to miracles is similar with the approach of liberal theologian Schleiermacher. Friedrich Daniel Ernst Schleiermacher (1768-1834), Professor at Halle (1804) and Berlin

---

[206] Tha Lian Fai, "The Significance of Karl Barth's Understands of the Word of God for Contemporary Mizo Christianity" (M.Th. Thesis, Senate of Serampore College (University), 1999), 109.

[207] Karl Barth, *Church Dogmatics* I/1 (Edinburg: T&T Clark, 1936), 124-125.

[208] Zairema, *Kan Bible Hi*, 241. 'The right status' here means the rank of perfect fellowship between God and human beings in Eden garden before the fall of human beings.

[209] D. A. Black & D. S. Dockery, eds., *New Testament Criticism and Interpretation* (Grand Rapids, Michigan: Zondervan Publishing House, 1991), 82.

(1810), was recognized as the Father of liberal German Theology in the nineteenth century, and most of his work on that field. His liberalism was different from the older rationalism of the Deist, and was strongly opposed to it. He combined a critical approach to textual and historical questions with a religious sensibility inherited from pietism. In his speeches on religion (1799), he argued that religion was the study of the non-rational side of human beings, which was just as important as the rational side, and that Christianity was the highest form of religion which had yet evolved. He was the first person to lecture on the life the historical Jesus, but his thoughts on the subject were not published until 1864, when they were severely criticized by Strauss. In his own lifetime, he published little in the Field of New Testament studies, apart from commentaries on 1 Timothy (1807) and Luke (1817).[210] From the aspect of 'Higher Biblical criticism' which was promoted by Enlightenment period,[211] Schleiermacher critically studies the Bible from the scientific doctrine. If it was scientifically true he would not shy away from declining Jesus' miracles.[212] Zairema also frequently used his scientific thinking for studying the Bible, especially the miracles. He first studied the doubts that

---

[210] Gerald Bray, *Biblical Interpretation: Past and Present* (England: APOLLOS, 1996), 326.

[211] An Age of Enlightenment (or simply the Enlightenment or Age of Reason) was a cultural movement of intellectuals in 18th century Europe, that sought to mobilize the power of reason, in order to reform society and advance knowledge. It promoted science and intellectual interchange and opposed superstition, intolerance and abuses in church and state. Originating about 1650 to 1700, it was sparked by philosophers Baruch Spinoza (1632–1677), John Locke (1632–1704), Pierre Bayle (1647–1706), mathematician Isaac Newton (1643–1727), and historian Voltaire (1694–1778). The wide distribution of the printing press, invented in Europe in 1440, made possible the rapid dispersion of knowledge and ideas which precipitated the Enlightenment. Ruling princes often endorsed and fostered figures and even attempted to apply their ideas of government in what was known as Enlightened Despotism. The Enlightenment flourished until about 1790–1800, after which the emphasis on reason gave way to Romanticism's emphasis on emotion and a Counter-Enlightenment gained force. "Age of Enlightenment," http://en.wikipedia.org/wiki/Age_of_Enlightenment. (3 Mar. 2012).

[212] Zirsangliana, *Theology Kalphung,* 74.

could be raised from the text, but at the same time tried to see the glory of God beyond the miracles. It seems that when he read the Bible, Zairema tried to see what the purpose of God was to human life. There are so many miracles mentioned in the Bible, yet the author of each book would point out the specific reason why they mentioned them. Zairema was afraid that people would fail to grasp the purpose of the message wherever one reads the miracle stories. He believes that people should attempt to understand the providence of God and find out the main aim of the messages instead of recognizing God as a magician.[213] Since Jesus tries to see the glory of God from simple things, Zairema urged us that we learn from Jesus. Jesus probably observed yeast altering the bread while watching his mother preparing bread, thus he could integrate this knowledge and compared it to the work of God in human life. When Jesus saw the dead body of sparrow, he realised that the programme of God was upon it and that God had also cared for every crow. When he saw the lilies of the field, he found the careful nursing of God. Many sowers sow the seeds without any thought of God's act, but Jesus always found the act of God (Mt. 6:25-34; 13:1-23, 33). Many people saw Jesus' miracles during his earthly life, but they did not believe him. Therefore, Jesus realized that miracles are not the reason of believing in him, if it is the cause of believing in God he would have done much more miracles. It teaches us that we should not try to see the glory of God from miraculous things. Rather, Zairema was very much concerned with seeking the purpose of what the message of the Bible was in simple things.[214] Many Mizo Christians seek the glory of God only from the miraculous things; they stress the miracles rather than the purpose of God's message in it. And they are depending upon miraculous incidents for their spiritual development and soon doubt God when miracles are out of sight. Therefore, it seems that Zairema's teaching of miracle is essential and reliable norm for our spiritual development and is truly God's purpose.

---

[213] Zairema, *Kan Bible Hi*, 259.

[214] Zairema, *Kan Bible Hi*, 271-272.

3) Bible is the Book Inspired by God: Zairema's acceptance of 'inspiration of God' is different from the acceptance of some evangelical groups. He opined that inspiration as in biblical inspiration is different from the inspiration found in the Biblical passage of Gen. 2:7: 'LORD God formed man from the dust of the ground, and breathed into his nostrils the breath of life; and the man became a living being.' The meaning of inspiration is not 'God inspired the Scriptures by breathing and it became a living word,' but it should meant that the Word is 'coming from God.'[215] Zairema believes that there is no other book in the world than the Bible which deeply touches the human hearts. We receive strength, comfort and knowledge about God from the Bible; this thought is not available in liberal thinking.[216] He used to say that reading the Bible is truly amazing; it gives that astuteness to the reader and union with God is intelligence.[217] If the readers make use of the Bible in their everyday life they will realise unfathomably that it is the word of God.[218] Zairema says that God also inspired the translation work. He goes on to write:

> As we participated in the translation work of the whole Bible, even if we add our own ideas and understandings in the translation, it may say sound astounding as it comes from the outside. Although, we have more initiative in the translation work, we realised that that to go beyond certain belief was not our own idea. Therefore, we accept Bible translation as an inspiration from God. At the same time, if we say that God tells us how to translate it, we would be a liar. If we say that without telling God we translated it, we will be a deceiver too.[219]

In the meantime Zairema used to say that verbal inspiration is unacceptable for the authority of the Bible. The original meaning of

---

[215] Zairema, *Kan Bible Hi*, 212.

[216] Zairema, *Kan Bible Hi*, 219.

[217] Zairema, *Kan Bible Hi*, 247.

[218] Zairema, *Kan Bible Hi*, 233.

[219] Zairema, *Kan Bible Hi*, 220.

Infallible, according to Zairema is, for the book, it means 'there is no pretence.' If it is for the Bible the original meaning indicates that 'the truthfulness of the Biblical passages and the truth is written in the Bible.' Due to the increasing of the meaning we are doubtful for that.[220] The first article of the Confession of Faith of PCI has the Bible as the 'infallible rule of faith and duty.' Many Mizo understood this as inerrancy of every word and sentences of the Bible.[221] Although, Mizo Christians, especially Presbyterian Church are already taught the relevance of Dynamic inspiration or Organic inspiration rather than Verbal inspiration since the 1999 adult Sunday School lesson,[222] yet many already had preconceived notion regarding the meaning of the 'inspiration of God,' they find it hard to accept the relevance of Dynamic inspiration or Organic inspiration. Zairema's deliberation of God's inspiration is quite credible for understanding the Inspiration. There are a variety of views of inspiration. Of these views, those that hold to any type of verbal dictation, the view that the very words of scripture were dictated by God, would be incompatible with the historical critical method.

In his contextual and indigenous expression Zairema was in favour to apply the early Mizo religious practices for amplification of the theology of salvation. Rodinmawia Ralte rightly supports Zairema's thought, and then he argued that the differentiation of

---

[220] Zairema, *Lehkhabu Te Pasarih*, 16&17.

[221] Rosiamliana Tochhawng, *A Study of Ten Articles of Faith of the Presbyterian Church of India* (Delhi: ISPCK, 2007), 41 (Hereafter will be cited as Tochhawng, *A Study of Ten Articles of Faith…,*). The *Nilai leh Beihrual Thupui* 2002 (The book is meant for Christian Education book to be studied every Wednesday night and during the Christian endeavor programme in the month of September) of the Mizoram Presbyterian Church, which was written by Revd Chuauthuama publicly set on fire by C. Lakhuma s/o C. Rualkhuma on 11th January 2002, the date that is celebrated as the Day of the Arrival of the Gospel, complaining that it contradicts against the Article No. 1 of Ten Articles of Faith of the PCI. The book deals with miracles in the OT using historical-critical method. That matter was taken up in the Executive Committee, which issued a circular concerning it. *Minutes of the 185th Synod Executive Committee of the Mizoram Presbyterian Church,* February 6-8, 2002, p. 19. Cited by Tochhawng, *A Study of Ten Articles of Faith,* 41.

[222] Lalsawma, *Kristian Thurin Zirna (A Study of Christian Theology)* (Aizawl: SL&PB, 1998), 11-12.

sacred portion and secular realm is never Mizo religious identity. Religious, economics, social and politics are clapped together as one in the early Mizo society.[223] But now a day, due to the differentiation of sacred and secular part, religiosity cannot deeply touch the mundane reality of the people. In the sense that Mizo understanding of salvation also needs make over and it is possible to make use of Mizo *Thangchhuah* concept for elaboration of Christ salvific work.

Since he worked on the religion of Lushais (Mizo) in his BD thesis, Zairema made use of many religious rites in interpreting Mizo theology. He gave high regards to the concept of Mizo *Thangchhuah* practices and their valuable contribution and sharing of their possessions to the community for uplifting the poor. He made use of them for the interpretation of Mizo's liberation theology.[224] Those who are generous for the poor, unselfish and are willing to be a blessing for other are able to perform *Thangchhuah*.[225]

The early Mizo believed in the continuance of life beyond death. Only souls of the rich and skillful hunters known as "*Thangchhuah,*" could enter *Pialral (Paradise)* as they would not have to work anymore, but would enjoy a plentitude of rice. Literally, "*Thang*" stands for 'famous' and '*Chhuah*' stands for 'accomplished.' The word *Thangchhuah* is perhaps derived from *Thangkim* (all famous). There are two forms of *Thangchhuah* viz. *In lama Thangchhuah (accomplished of domestic task)* and *Ram lama Thangchhuah* (*accomplished of jungle*

---

[223] Rodinmawia Ralte "Mizo Pi Pute Thlarau Khawthlir Hmanga Mizo Kristian Siam That" in *Zoram Thar A Awm Thei Ang Em?* Edited by L. H. Rawsea et al. (Bangalore: Bangalore Mizo Association, 2011), 176. Rodinmawia Ralte is an ordained minister, a scholar in the department of Religion and is teaching Religion subject in the Academy of Integrated Christian Studies (AICS) Mizoram, (Hereafter will be cited as Rodinmawia Ralte, "Mizo Pi Pute Thlarau Khawthlir,").

[224] See Zairema, *Pi Pute Biak Hi*, 124 & 171.

[225] Kipgen also says that, it was for this reason that the community accorded *Thangchhuahpa* great respect and honour. They believed his position had been achieved by the blessings of God to whom they had offered the prescribed sacrifices without fail Mangkhosat Kipgen, *Christianity and Mizo Culture: The Encounter Between Christianity and Zo Culture in Mizoram* (Aizawl: Mizo Theological Conference, 1997), 124.

task).[226] *Thangchhuah* could be attained either by performing *Ram lama Thangchhuah (Thangchhuah* at forest*)*, in which case a person distinguished himself by killing certain prescribed animals and performed a series of feasts. The list of animals that a person had to kill were one each of the following species of animals such as barking deer (*sakhi*), sāmbhar (*sazuk/zukchal*), bear (*savawm*), wild boar (*sanghal*), wild mythun/gayal (*ramsial*), and elephant (*sai*).[227] Besides these animals, one must also kill a king cobra (*rulngân*), a flying lemur (*vahluk*), and an eagle (*muvanlai*) to gain greater honor.[228] They also had to perform a ceremony called "Ai" for eating animal they had slaughtered so that these animals might be their salves in the life after death.

The other method was called *In lama Thangchhuah* (*Thangchhuah* at home); to earn this, one had to provide give a series of feasts to the whole village. The purpose of performing this feast was also to re-distribute wealth to the less fortunate without any feeling. For *In lama Thangchhuah*, they should follow the ceremonial feast for the community. This community feast was done by the worship of *Khua* (the sustainer of community lives). Due to space limitation, the order of ceremonial feasts for *In lama Thangchhuah* will be mentioned without further explanation - 1) *Sakung,* 2) *Chawng (Chawn), 3) Dawino Chhui, 4) Sedawi, 5) Sekhuan and mitthi rawp lâm 6) Khuangchawi.*[229] Not only of the community of the village, but also of the relatives from nearby villages participate at the feasts which had caused the feasts very expensive. The *Thangchhuah* was expected to continue providing the feast even after he had completed *Khuangchawi* feast. Therefore he would perform *Khuangchawi* even twice or thrice, going through the whole series of feasts again. Those who had completed providing the feasts for three times were called *Zaudawh* and the provider were called *Zawhzawzo* (who had

[226] V. S. Lalrinawma, *Mizo Ethos: Changes and Challenges* (Aizawl: Mizoram Publication Board, 2005), 107.

[227] Zairema, *Pi Pute Biak Hi…*, 60.

[228] J. Shakespeare, *The Lushei Kuki Clans, Part-I*, (Aizawl: Tribal Research Institute, 1975), 63.

[229] B. Lalthangliana, *India, Burma & Bangladesh-a Mizo Chanchin* (Aizawl: Remkungi, 2001), 333-348.

finished all the rites demanded for human).[230] The requirements to become *Zawhzawzo* was too expensive that it was difficult for every *Thangchhuah* to attain this position.[231]

The early Mizo believed in the existence of life after death. Only souls of the rich and skillful hunters known as "*Thangchhuah,*" could enter *Pialral* where they would not need to work for survival but enjoy life with plentiful ready foodstuffs.[232] Everyone who had died had to pass through a place called *Pawla Kawt* (*Pawla's* street). It was impossible for every soul to avoid him as there was no route for escape. Pawla used to shoot at the ankle bone of the souls who passed through him with big pellets of his catapult, except those who died of in infancy called *hlamzuih,* virgins, *tlangval nula* ***'ngai'***[233] *and Thangchhuah* couples. Those who got hit by *Pawla's* pellet couldn't reach *Pialral* and were doomed to stay in *Mitthi khua* (dead men's village), where they live a dreamlike life but similar to the earthly lifestyle. Those who escaped the pellet of *Pawla* could freely enter in to *Pialral* (the last spiritual abode). While crossing the street of *Pawla* the *Thangchhuahpa* will ride the elephant[234] and hold the horns of sāmbhar, the king cobra (rulngân) loosely wraps itself around him and the horns. An eagle (*muvanlail*) would try to seize the king cobra

---

[230] Zairema, *Pi Pute Biak Hi...,* 58.

[231] Malsawmdawngliana, "*Thangchhuah* Feasts and Their Implications in Mizo Society" *Man in India,* Vol. 89, Nos. 1-2 (Jan.-June 2009): 236. *Thangchhuahpa* was entitled to various privileges such as: 1) To open windows in his side wall according to his pleasure, 2) To create dividing walls in his house. 3) To construct his house with *Vanlung* (or veranda). 4) To wear a special distinctively designed cloth, known as *Thangchhuah puan.* 5) To wear a special kind of turban (*Dartial).* 6) To enter *Pialral* (or Paradise) directly {K. Zawla, *Mizo Pi Pute leh An Thlahte Chanchin...,* 31}.

[232] Zairema said that besides *Thangchhuah, hlamzuih* (died during infancy) and virgin are able to enter in the Pialral. {Zairema, *Pi Pute Biak Hi...,*31}.

[233] *Tlangval nula* ***'ngai'*** should means a bachelor who was a religious person or who high regards the ritual of their religion, '*Ngai'* is not 'sexual intercourse' but it was a sacred language {see, Zairem, *Pi Pute Biak Hi...,* 123 & B. Lalthangliana, *India, Burma & Bangladesh-a Mizo Chanchin...,* 336}.

[234] If they killed elephant they will sit on it. It seems that killing of elephant is not compulsory, some books says that *Thangchhuahpa* will sit on the Sāmbhar. (see B. Lalthangliana, *India, Burma & Bangladesh-a Mizo Chanchin...,* 352).

(*rulngan*) but the *Thangchhuah* could drive them off and he will be shaded by flying lemur (*vahluk*) flying above him. *Thangchhuahpa* will be followed by all who were destined to be his slaves such as all the other animals he had killed and also all the men he killed in wars. Seeing the boastful self-presentation of the *Thangchhuahpa*, even the frightful *Pawla* would not dare to shoot him with his catapult but rather give him free passage to reach *Pialral*.[235]

When we look at the role of *Thangchhuahpa* every stage of the ceremonial feast for the *In lama Thangchhuah* was also an occasion when the poor and the hungry could share in the bounty. Every *Thangchhuahpa* would try to perform *Khuangchawi* feast at least thrice in a lifetime even though this was very expensive. The reason of *Sechhun Khuangchawi* is not only enjoyment of a plentitude of rice and providing at free cost without any hard labor but also to distribute their possessions to the poor people in the community. During the day of *Khuangchawi, Khuangchawinu* (wife of the patron) threw up their valuable possessions like, staff (for a token of gun), money coins, rope (for a token of mithun), chicken etc. The main purpose was to distribute the wealth of the rich to the poor without any guilty feeling. For the Mizo there was no greater virtue than an act of bravery and generosity that serves the welfare of the people even if the cost of that feast was very high.[236]

For *Ram lama Thangchhuah*, the purpose was sacrificing their life for their fellow villagers specially to prevent their crops destructive animals. When the hunter prepared the feast ceremony called '*Ai*' for the slaugtered animals, the poor people also participate in the feast.[237] This shows that the *Thangchhuahpa* is a kind hearted, unselfish, generous and brave person. Liberation from wild beast and enemies and upliftment of the downtrodden people from their economic and social slavery are the important roles of *Thangchhuahpa*.

---

[235] J. Shakespeare, *The Lushei Kuki Clans, Part–I...*, 63.

[236] Liangkhaia, *Mizo Chanchin,* 4th edition, (Aizawl: Mizo Academy of Letters,1976), 12.

[237] Mangkhosat Kipgen, *Christianity and Mizo Culture: The Encounter Between Christianity and Zo Culture in Mizoram* (Aizawl: Mizo Theological Conference, 1997), 123.

According to Zairema, "Those who could perform *Thangchhuah* are abstemious persons, and never became disruptive for the community. It seems that their incorruptibility for the community is the reason for their direct access to *Pialral*."[238] While the general belief affirned that the Thangchhuah and the brave persons who dare hit a wooden post called *Thingserh* with their dao (sword) to show that they are ready to die for the community will have direct access to *Pialrâl*. Zairema remarkably argued that even some persons, like Taitesena, who oractically lived their lives with the concept of *tlawmngaihna* also might have direct access to *Pialrâl*.[239]

Being a communitarian society, each individual person was bounded by the community. Individualism has little room in Mizo society. Each individual person focuses on community service and well being, and the one who rendered most and noblest service to the community was highly rewarded. *Thangchhuah* persons both *In lama Thangchhuah* and *Ram lama Thangchhuah* are a man of orthopraxis than orthodoxy, talked less and did more, set an exemplary life for others through courageous acts, high moral and noble lives. They applied Mizo ethical teaching, '*sem sem dam dam ei bil thi thi*.'[240] When they shot the animals they used to distribute the meat as equally as possible to whom who came in the locus and sometimes they used to distribute to all the villagers. At that time the surplus for the killer was only the head of the animals. It can be said that *Thangchhuah* lived and died for others, surrenderes their days for the community. Through their untiring service and dedication *Thangchhuahpa* can be regarded as a 'man for others.'

The life of the *Thangchhuah* was an extraordinary life since their life was not only marked by skills of hunting and wealth but also marked by their self-sacrificial services to the ordinary people i.e., self-emtied life. As we know that for *Ram lama Thangchhuah*,

---

[238] Zairema, *Pi Pute Biak Hi ...*, 124.

[239] Zairema, *Pi Pute Biak Hi,...*, 31.

[240] *Sem sem dam dam, ei bil thi thi* literally means 'those who hoard dies but who share alive,' 'as long as you share you live, eating everything alone will die.'

there are various prescribed animals to be killed whick were very obstructive for their life and jhum caltivation.[241]

In lama Thangchhuah is also impossible for selfish and stingy persons and those who do not have much concern for others. It demanded to prepare banquet so many times for the community. One could become a *'In lama Thangchuah'* by giving at least four public feasts in prescribed order.[242] The poor people used to take the rice from their rice bin. However, Zairema was of the opinion that *Thangchhuah* required sharing of wealth with the poor and the act of Charity but not many people did so. To achieve the ceremonies of *Thangchhuah, Sechhun Khuangchawi* was very expensive. It requires 100 ngân (around 1500 kg) of rice beer (zu) and they used around 1800 kgs (*phur sawmthum in* Mizo measurement) of rice for beer. They used to expend more than half of their stocked rice for feast.[243] In the second day called 'Zupui Ni' of the *Sechhun Khuangchawi*, there was a time in the evening for a special act called "*Buh Thai.*" The *Khuangchawi* person used to heap up their rice in their floor which would be scratched down from the hole so that the rice could be collected by the poor and that rice could sometime amount to 180 kgs (*phur thum* in Mizo measurement).[244]

As Rodinmawia Ralte asserts that the essential part for the way of salvation (which means entering *Pialral*), which was done by *Thangchhuahpa/nu* is emptying himself and blessings for others. The kernel of the Mizo religious pilgrimage is *"I will bless you...so that you will be a blessing"* (Gen 12.2).[245] As Kipgen says that it was for this reason that the community accorded him great respect and honor.

---

[241] Zairema, *Pi Pute Biak Hi...,* 171.

[242] Zairema, "The Mizos and their Religion" in *Towards a Tribal Theology The Mizo Perspective*, edited by K. Thanzauva (Aizawl: Mizo Theological Conference, 1989), 41-42.

[243] Zairema, *Pi Pute Biak Hi...,* 58.

[244] Zairema, *Pi Pute Biak Hi...,* 42.

[245] Rodinmawia Ralte, "Mizo Pi Pute Thlarau Khawthlir Hmanga Mizo Kristian Siam That" in *Zoram Thar A Awm Thei Ang Em?* (Bangalore: Bangalore Mizo Association, 2011), 178-179.

They believed his position had been achieved by the blessings of God to whom they had offered the prescribed sacrifices without fail.[246]

According to Zairema, for the achievement of *In lama Thangchhuah*, in all of the ways of *Thangchuah* the central ceremony was the sacrifice of the '*Sial* (mythun) to '*Khua*' also called '*Sechhun*.' Although, it was a sacrifice made by individual (the patron), the whole village was involved.[247] So, many numbers of mythun will be killed for worshipping *Khua/Khuavang* (one of the gods of Mizo, it is equivalent to *Pathian*[248]) *for the community.*[249] *The role of Thangchhuah* became more and more important because these ceremonies and the consequent spiritual benefits became the protectors for the hunters and providers for the village community.

Schleiermacher proposed that Christ - the Arche-type. To him, the redeemer is active in us, as God is active in him, we are passive in regard to him, as he is passive in his humanity in regard to God. His redemptive activity is the work of God through him in us.[250] Christ as the supreme model of Christian discipleship and he is Christ the Savior and Christ the example (1 Pet 2.21,24), Christ for us and Christ in us, and call to follow Christ both in withdrawal and in involvement.[251] One of the reasons of Jesus' coming is to present abundant life to human (Jn 10.10). This abundant life means true life, quality of and extraordinary life[252] which is to be presented

---

[246] Mangkhosat Kipgen, *Christianity and Mizo Culture: The Encounter Between Christianity and Zo Culture in Mizoram* (Aizawl: Mizo Theological Conference, 1997), 124.

[247] Zairema, "The Mizos and their Religion" in *Towards a Tribal Theology The Mizo Perspective*, edited by K. Thanzauva (Aizawl: Mizo Theological Conference, 1989), 41-42.

[248] Zairema, *Pi Pute Biak Hi…,* 199.

[249] Zairema, *Pi Pute Biak Hi…,* 59.

[250] Lalnghakthuami, *Lecture Note on Person and Work of Christ*, nd. & np., 64.

[251] John Stott, *The Incomparable Christ* (Secunderabad: OM-Authentic Books, 2001), 64, 67.

[252] In Greek word 'abundant life' is *zoen perisson, perrison* coming from *perissos* (Adj/noun) which means extraordinary, abundant, unnecessary and advantage. {R. Chhuanliana, *Greek-Mizo Lexicon (Layman's Guide to the New Testament Greek Grammer and Lexicon)* (Aizawl: Lengchhawn Press, 2007), 288.}

to others and to bear much fruit (Jn 15.16). When we look at all the involvements of *Thangchhuahpa*, they liberated psychological entrapment of the poor people through their generosity; they set an example to eradicate close-handedness through the feasts and so on. Just like Jesus' life was bounded by love, care, kindness, peace, comfort etc., *Thangchhuah* life was also tied up with *Mizo tlawmngaihna* (selfless sacrifice). They were a comforter and a very present help in trouble for the needy persons in economically and psychologically. So, they were an ethical exemplar among the Mizo. In this way, Zairema made use the primitive Mizo religion for implementing the salvific work of Christ.

Besides these, Zairema realized that the importance of culture and language and he makes use Mizo primitive religion for implementing theology. He clearly mentioned his thought in his articles, "Sakhua leh Culture (Religion and Culture)," and "A Quest for Indigenous Expression of Christian Theology."[253] His approach is closely related with George A. Lindbeck's[254] model of 'Cultural-Linguistic Alternative.' In Lindbeck's model, Cultural-Linguistic Alternative is preferable to traditional cognitivist and experiential-expressive approaches, provided the aim is to give a non-theological account of the relations of religion and experience.[255] According to Lindbeck, a religion can be viewed as a kind of cultural and/or linguistic framework or medium that shapes the entirety of life

---

[253] Zairema, *Thukhawchang Mi Pekte Hi*, 112-123, 170-184.

[254] George A. Lindbeck is one of the America's leading systematic theologians. He seeks to construct a new basis for Christian theology. He is Pitkin Professor of Historical Theology at Yale University.

[255] George A. Lindbeck, *The Nature of Doctrine: Religion and Theology in a Postliberal Age* (London: SPCK, 1984), 30. (Hereafter will be cited as Lindbeck, *The Nature of Doctrine:,*). This model understands religions as idioms for dealing with whatever is most important – with ultimate questions of life and death, right and wrong, chaos and order, meaning and meaningless. These are the problems they treat rites, instruction, and order socializing processes, not only on the conscious mind but in the individual and cultural subconscious. Lindbeck, *The Nature of Doctrine:,* 40. The description of this model is shaped by the ultimate theological concerns of the present inquiry, but it is consonant, with the anthropological, sociological, and philosophical studies by which it has been for the most part inspired. Lindbeck, *The Nature of Doctrine:,* 32.

and thought. For Lindbeck, just as a language is correlated with a form of life, and just as a culture has both cognitive and behaviour dimensions, so it is also in the case of a religious tradition. Its doctrines, cosmic stories or myths, and ethical directives are integrally related to the rituals it practices, the sentiments or experiences it evokes, the actions it recommends, and the institutional forms it develops.[256] As Thomas Harvey pointed out that this model doesn't necessarily deny the ontological truth of doctrine or the importance of how people experience the divine. Rather, it argues that these truths and experience need to be understood culturally and linguistically; viz., that doctrine is a form of cultural linguistic activity to establish and therefore should not be artificially isolated from the rest of human sociocultural activity. Thus, according to Lindbeck, doctrine functions as a sort of grammar that distinguishes specific Christian cultures from each other as well as other religions in terms of the orientation of life and practices by any given Christian community. Thomas continues to say that the strength of this model is its recognition of the situated nature and definition of truth and heresy.[257] Zairema was in favour of this model to make use for the instrument of contextual theology.

Liberative

Zairema says, "The salvific work of Christ would not be meaningful if it does not touch the mundane reality of their lives. The theology of liberation was developed in order to address their situation."[258] In India the high caste people always dominated the outcaste people for thousands of years; they treated them like dogs. Although, some Hindu people considered it wrong, no one really cares to save them from their entrapment. Because God never likes an abject state of poverty for the people, God made use of the British government, Mahatma Gandhi, Dr. Ambedkar and Jawaharlal Nehru for their

[256] Lindbeck says that all this is involved in comparing a religion to a cultural-linguistic system. Lindbeck, *The Nature of Doctrine:*, 33.

[257] Thomas Harvey, "Heresy Reconsidered: Why the Non-Western World is Rediscovering the Necessity of Theological and Ecclesial Definition," *Mizoram Theological Journal,* XI & XII/3 (July–December, 2005): 36.

[258] Zairema, "A Quest for Indigenous Expression, 120.

uplift from the degrading conditions.[259] We can say that Zairema's theology of Salvation is very Calvinist because Calvin's' theology, including his doctrine of God, is addressed to socio-political and economic context.[260] We can say that the necessity of empowerment of liberation theology always binds his whole life. He was very much concerned with good relationship among human beings and he realized that righteousness and reverence to each other is the instrument of human dignity.

Since he was very familiar with Hebrew and Greek language, Zairema's theological implications are very biblical and reliable. His co-worker Lalbiaktluanga says that when they translated the Bible, Zairema persistently learned the root word and background of the text, and only then could they set out as relevantly as possible for the Mizo.[261] If we carefully study his theology of salvation, we can understand his self-belief about the text. His theology of salvation clearly shows his liberative aspect of biblical hermeneutics and we can come to know that is the way how he read the Bible. Since we need to know his biblical approach, we will look at his theological implications about salvation as the followings:

1) Sin and Salvation: A simple definition of sin from the early Christian till today is 'aversion from God and conversion to creature' (*aversio a Deo et conversio ad creaturam*) (cf. Rom 1:21-25).[262] According to Zairema, the main cause of human's fall is the desire of equal status with God, wanting of supremacy over his/her fellow human beings, pride and self-centredness, and the forsaking of the love and goodness of God. He says that if we try to define the meaning of sin, there can be several definitions, but the basic

---

[259] Zairema, *Kan Bible HI,* 276-277.

[260] H. Vanlalauva, *Doctrine of God: John Calvin's Doctrine of God With Special Reference to the Indian Context* (Delhi: ISCPK, 2006), 279. (Hereafter will be cited as Vanlalauva, *Doctrine of God,*).

[261] Interview with Lalbiaktluanga, on 21st.12.2011 on his residence, Bungkawn Tlang veng, Aizawl. He is an ordained minister under the Mizoram Presbyterian Church Synod and a former Moderator & Bible translator and co-worker of Zairema in the Bible translation work.

[262] H. Vanlalauva & Rosiamliana Tochhawng, *Kristian Theology* (Aizawl: Aizawl Theological College, 2004), 89.

meaning is wanting of superiority and pride. The wishful thinking of mortal is to be equivalent with God, and if possible, human natures always like to be supreme even over God. Since human nature wants to rule over his/her fellow human being, many evils have broken out. Since he/she likes to have power over to his/her fellow human being, there cannot be mutual relationship. At this juncture there cannot be sweet communion with God.[263]

H. Vanlalauva thinks that Zairema's understanding of salvation is "fulfilment of the purpose," or "Return to innocence."[264] Salvation is the re-creation of the fallen humankind and from its negative consequences. Zairema pointed out the definition of the meaning of sin in the Hebrew word *het,' hatta't* and Greek word *hamartia,* which means "to miss the mark,"[265] or failure to reach a goal.[266] Sin is the failure to fulfil ones' obligations (Gen. 31:36; 42:22),[267] or 'falling short of one's true nature.'[268] Zairema said that Jesus, who had fulfilled God's purpose in him, even though fully human, could work miracles; if human beings also fulfilled the purpose they can do anything as Jesus did. Jesus himself clearly mentioned: "the one who believes in me will also do the works that I do and, in fact, will do greater works than these" (John 14:12).[269] Although, the Bible says that human beings are created in the image of God, we cannot know the real nature of human beings. Owing to the limitation of human knowledge, we cannot fully know the reality of soul and spirit in our body.

---

[263] Zairema, *Kan Bible Hi,* 283.

[264] Vanlalauva, "Rev. Dr. Zairema'n Chhandamna a Kapui Dan, 9. "return to innocence" here means the right position of human being before the fall, before the fall there was mutual relationship between God and human beings. This status is shared for the believers.

[265] John L. McKenzie, *Dictionary of the Bible* (Bangalore: Asian Trading Corporation, 2002), 817. (Hereafter will be cited as McKenzie, *Dictionary of the Bible,*).

[266] Stephen J. Duffy, "Sin," *The New Dictionary of Catholic Spatiality,* edited by Michael Downey (Bangalore: Theological Publication in India, 2003), 889-901.

[267] McKenzie, *Dictionary of the Bible,* 817.

[268] Vanlalauva, "Rev. Dr. Zairema'n Chhandamna a Kalpui Dan, 9.

[269] Zairema, *Kan Bible Hi,* 270.

Zairema pointed out that the salvation of God includes all spheres of human life including cosmos. While we may boast because we have the assurance of salvation, and yet the whole creation has been groaning in labour pains (cf. Rom 8:18-25), our salvation is not completed. Zairema strongly opined that God's salvific work is in process before becoming complete. Freedom of other creations from bondage to decay is the completion of God's salvation. In this sense Zairema said that those who are being saved through the cross of Christ cannot take rest. Because the creation is suffering, many people are also struggling for daily their needs. So, salvation includes all aspects of humankinds.[270] In the mean time, it is different from the stand point of some Mizo Christians who maintain that their personal and vision is much more important than what the Bible says to them. Some even believe that the Bible is unnecessary.[271] From the view of Evangelical theology, salvation is the change of position before God, from guilty to innocent.[272] Many Mizo Christians also understand that salvation is individual and includes only soul saving. They seldom understand salvation as corporate which includes other creatures. Their understanding of salvation appears to contradict Zairema's approach the Bible in this case. Even though from the Evangelical Theology, Zairema's approach is too liberal and difficult to accept and many could not understand his biblical approach, yet when we critically analyse Zairema's understanding, it seems that it is quite practicable and very lasting.

From the tribal perspective of the concept of God-Human-World, Zairema's theology of salvation is quite relevant. A tribal holistic concept of reality emphasizes the inter-relatedness of all things, against dualism.[273] It challenges anthropocentric theology

---

[270] Zairema, *Isua Rilru,* 232.

[271] H. Vanlalauva, "Thurin leh Zirtirna Lama Mizo Kristiate Harsatna," in *Kum 100 Kristian Zofate Hmabak (Task Ahead for a 100 years Old Mizo Christian),* edited by R. L. Rinawma, et al. (Bangalore: Bangalore Mizo Christian Fellowship, 1994), 7.

[272] H. Wayne House, *Charts of Christian Theology and Doctrine* (Grand Rapids, Michigan: Zondervan Publishing House, 1992), 92. (Hereafter will be cited as House, *Charts of Christian,*).

[273] Thanzauva, *Theology of Community*, 167.

which limits salvation to human being alone. The concept of God-Human-World challenges us to revise our understanding of salvation. This would lead us to broaden the circle of salvation from salvation of individual souls for life after death to understanding of cosmic salvation – the total salvation of human beings with their body, soul, spirit, society and all other creatures as well, here and now and in the future.[274] From the perspective of liberative aspect, sin is defined as anything which discriminates it, especially from the perspective of Feminist hermeneutics, structural violence, anything without promoting dignity, equality and fraternity is sin. In view of the fact that Zairema's biblical hermeneutics includes liberation from every entrapment of humankinds and he was concerned with abolishing any oppressive structures, his view is quite relevant from liberative aspects.

2) Redemption: Redemption,[275] according to Zairema, is one of the important interpretations for salvation. Zairema emphasized

---

[274] Thanzauva, *Theology of Community*, 167.

[275] The word redemption is in Hebrew *'goel,'* which means to express the action of a relative in setting free a member of his family or buying back his property (Lev 25:25ff.) or in general that of purchasing something for a price. A ransom-price is paid to secure the release of what would otherwise be under forfeit (e.g. Exod 21:30). Religiously God acts as redeemer by powerfully delivering his people from captivity (Exod 6:6-7; Isa 48:20) or even from sin (Ps 130:8). A ransom may also be paid to God in the form of a sacrifice or offering, to deliver people whose lives would otherwise be forfeit (Exod 13:13). I. H. Marshall, "Redemption," *New Dictionary of Theology*, edited by Sinclair B. Ferguson, et al., 1988, Reprint (Leicester, England: Inter- Varsity Press, 2005), 560. For the secular realm redemption is best to begin with the participle *'goel.' Goel* is used of a man's nearest relative at a particular time. In Lev 25:48f., it refers to a man's brother, uncle, cousin, or some other kinsman who is responsible for standing up for him and maintaining his rights. The following specific cases are mentioned in the OT:

a) If someone sells a house or a piece of property to pay a debt, there is a right of redemption (*ge'ullah*), and the nearest relative at the time is bound to buy back that which was sold and thus restore the possession of the family (Lev 25:25-34; Jer 32:6f.)The book of Ruth contains an example: Boaz is the *go'el* of Naomi and Ruth (2:20); but there is a nearer kinsman who has the priority (3:12; 4:4). He is quite willing to buy the piece of property, but not to marry Ruth as well (which apparently was a part of the responsibilities accruing to the *ge'ullah*, 4:4-6). But Boaz accepts both responsibilities (4:9f). In this instance, the legal ramifications are a little complicated, and cannot be explained in all details. b) If Israelite sold

redemption as one of the appropriate and relevant terms for defining salvation for the Mizo Christian, because some of the Mizo chiefs were enslaved by the *Pawih* people of eastern Mizoram. They would demand a ransom of 40 mithuns for the price of buying back those enslaved chiefs. If their family could give the demanded prices, they released them and the chiefs could continue their functions.[276] The popular display of the Bible for salvation is the Exodus event where God used Moses to save Israelites from the bondage of Egyptians. In this event, God is portrayed as "redeemer" (Heb. *Goel*). Zairema said, "YHWH is the God of Israelites and *Goel.* Their *Goel* saved them through Moses from the slavery of Egyptians so that they could live as normal human being."[277] Likewise, Babylonian exile also pondered upon God's redemptive work (Isa. 40:10). The released people of Israelite returned to their native place to live as they had before. This returning to the original status is called salvation which is mentioned in the Bible. Shabbat and Jubilee are also the salvific works which is returning to the people their rightful position. As human being are originally intended to be in the image and likeness of God, the main purpose of Jesus' salvific work through the cross is said fulfil that

himself to a foreign as a slave, the right of redemption by the *go'el* was also applicable (Lev 25:47-54). In this case, there was a breach in the whole nation that must be repaired. c) If someone is murdered, his death shall be avenged by the *go'el haddam*, "avenger of blood" whose responsibility is to kill the murderer or a member of his clan (*-naqam*). The avenger of blood is first of all dead man's son, and other male relatives (Num 35:12, 19-27; Dt. 1 9:6, 12; Josh 20:2f., 5,9). d) Lev 27 contains a case analogous to a and b: in certain cases described in detail, votive offerings that had been dedicated to the deity can be bought back by the original owner, but its value shall be increases by 20 % (vv 13,15,19,31). In one passage, Num 5:8, the *go'el* appears as a recipient of atonement money, and this, of course, in his role as responsible head of the family (clan). Some passages in which *go'el* is used in a figurative sense (Prov 23:11; Jer 50:34; Lam 3:58; Ps 119:154; Job 19:25) show that the *go'el* could appear as a helper in a lawsuit a *go'el* (RSV, "Kinsman") and a real (1 Kings 16:11) has no one who cares for his rights and honour. {G. Johannes Botterweck & Helmer Ringgren, eds., *Theological Dictionary of the Old Testament*, translated by John T. Willis, 1975, Reprint (Grand Rapids, Michigan: William B. Eerdmans Publishing Company, 1983), 352}.

[276] Zairema, *Kan Bible HI.*, 278.

[277] Zairema, *Kan Bible HI*, 277.

purpose which is to be the likeness of God.[278] Due to the work of sin, human beings lost their full humanity and mutual relationship with God in the Garden of Eden. Therefore, in the light of Zairema's teaching of redemption, the will of God to human is re-formulating that mutual relationship and to return to the original status. There is one of divergent theories of atonement in the early church which is 'The Ransom Paid to Satan Theory.'[279] But, it seems that Zairema did not try to follow that preconceived notion of definition and they contradicted each other. As H. Vanlalauva commended him, Zairema's definition of redemption is very much in line with biblical teaching.[280]

3) Fellowship and Eternal Life: In the light of Zairema's teaching, we can say that communion with God and eternal life is the same meaning. Zairema strongly opined that through the teaching of the Bible, the difference of life and death can be measured from whether one is having fellowship with God or not. The Bible says that without fellowship with God one is dead,[281] but at the same time, communion with God is life.[282] Zairema continues to say that this communion with God is called 'eternal life' and 'the life of God.' The main focus of Jesus' salvation is also fellowship with God. H. Vanlalauva asserts that this explanation has good connection with 'fulfilment of the purpose' and 'return to innocence' which is already mentioned above.[283] The communion with God resulted in becoming good fruits with our fellow human beings and in turn makes good relationship among human beings.

---

[278] Zairema, *Lehkhabu Te Pasarih*, 52.

[279] This Ransom to Satan Theory is based on the singular notion that the death of Christ constituted a ransom paid to Satan, in order to cancel the just claims which the latter had on human beings. Origen, one of the chief advocates of this theory, held that Satan was deceived in the bargain, since the outcome proved that he could not stand in the presence of the holy Christ, and was not able to retain his hold on Him. Louis Berkhof, *Introduction to Systematic Theology* (Grand Rapids, Michigan: Baker Book House, 1979), 384.

[280] Vanlalauva, "Rev. Dr. Zairema'n Chhandamna a Kalpui Dan, 10.

[281] Zairema, *Kan Bible Hi,* 273.

[282] Zairema, *Kan Bible Hi,* 282.

[283] Vanlalauva, "Rev. Dr. Zairema'n Chhandamna a Kalpui Dan, 11.

According to Zairema, "Heaven[284] lies in the relationship between human beings and human beings. It is invisible from outside but it is within human beings. If our heart is right, there can be sweet fellowship with God. When we say that our relationship with God is good, our relationship with our fellow human beings should also be good."[285] Zairema's understanding of heaven is divergent from Neo-Orthodox theology of God. According to Soren Kierkegaard, a Neo-Orthodox theologian, God is wholly transcendent except when God chooses to be revealed to human. God is totally sovereign over and free from God's creation. God cannot be known through proofs.[286] So, from the side of Neo-Orthodox theology, Zairema's teaching of fellowship with God and eternal life is impossible to accept. But, at the same time, it is quite reliable and significant for today Christian.

4) Original Sin: The traditional teaching of original sin, according to Berkhof is that sin entered the world as the result of the transgression of Adam and Eve in Eden Garden, a paradise. The first sin was occasioned by the temptation of Satan in the form of serpent, who sowed in human's heart the seeds of distrust and unbelief.[287] On the basis of Ps 51:5, Augustine defined Original sin as inherited sin; he considered that the fallen nature of Adam was transmitted

---

[284] Heaven, Kingdom of God and Eternal life are same, in the sense that Zairema indicated that heaven is the place where fellowship with God and the place of doing God's will (cf. Zairema, *Kan Bible Hi,* 281-282).

[285] Zairema, *Kan Bible Hi,* 281.

[286] House, *Charts of Christian,* 10.

[287] Scripture clearly indicates that the serpent, who appears as the tempter in the story of the Fall, was but an instrument of Satan (John 8:44; Rom 16: 20; 2 Cor 11:3; Rev 12:9). The first sin consisted in human's eating of the tree of the knowledge of good and evil. This eating was sinful simply because God had forbidden it. It clearly showed that human was not willing to subject his/her will unconditionally to the will of God, and comprised several elements. In the intellect it revealed itself as unbelief and pride, in the will as the desire to be like God, and in the affections as an unholy satisfaction in eating of the forbidden fruit. As a result of it human lost the image of God in the restricted sense, became guilty and utterly corrupt, and fell under the sway of death, (Gen 3:19; Rom 5:12; 6:23). Louis Berkhof, *A Summary of Christian Doctrine,* 1960, Reprint (Edinburgh: The Banner of the Truth Trust, 2002), 57.

biologically through sexual procreation.[288] Zairema did not accept Augustine's teaching of Original sin. He says that every human being infringed the order of God as we like it. We will bear the blame for our own sins. When he critically studied from the background and the root meaning, Zairema thought that the Psalmist just wrote about his personal infringement and it could not mean infant is born with sin. He said that there is no teaching of original sin in other OT books except Ps. 51:5. He opined that these biblical verses Jer 31:29, 30; Ezek 18:2-4 and Deut 24:16 contradict Original sin.[289] There is no Adam's sin which is transmitted biologically through sexual procreation in the Jewish tradition and in their religious teaching. When Jesus comments a man blind from birth, he said, "Neither this man nor his parents sinned; he was born blind so that God's works might be revealed in him." (Jn 9:3). The doctrine of Original sin is almost near Paul's teaching in the letter to Romans, "Therefore, just as sin came into the world through sin, and so death spread to all because all have sinned." (Rom 5:12). But, since the following verse (v. 14) says, "...even over those whose sins were not like the transgression of Adam," Zairema thought that the teaching that all died in Adam's death is not acceptable. For him, when we read Rom 1: 18-32, this verse does not match with Original sin. So, it seems that Paul also did not teach Original sin.[290] Zairema expressed his thought about the fall of human beings as such by saying that Gen 3:3 mentioned not physical death but spiritual death. If it was about physical death they will die just after they ate the fruit, but they were alive over seven hundred years (Gen 5:3-5). It seems the third chapter of Genesis is not the narration of Original sin or the beginning of the cause of all human's sin but the narration appears as an indication for that willingness in human's hearts to long for something which seems better. Zairema believes that this keenness to forsake the old practice and aim for a better position has indeed a 'price' which humans must

---

[288] J. E. Colwell, "Sin," *New Dictionary of Theology*, edited by Sinclair B. Ferguson, et al., 1988, Reprint (Leicester, England: InterVarsity Press, 2005), 642.

[289] Zairema, *Kan Bible Hi*, 261.

[290] Zairema, *Isua Rilru,* 229.

pay for.[291] Our body was created to be mortal; in other books of the Bible it says, "The days of our life are seventy years, or perhaps eighty, if we are strong;" (Ps 90:10).

Since all human beings are saturated completely by death due to sin, sin began from one person. And then sin envelops the whole community, therefore one becomes dead in the eyes of God.[292] Zairema believed that we are beings created like Adam even now in the image of God, so we can say, 'I myself am also created in the image of God.'[293] He continued to say that Adam is not a personal name but it means mortal, if we say that Adam has fallen, it should mean human has fallen. So, it seems we can say that there was disobedience to God since time immemorial by our ancestors. In each life there is an ability to obey God just like in the Eden Garden.[294] Zairema continues to assert that God had always creates the world by God's love but human beings continue to spoil it, humans are responsible for ruining what God had called 'good.' And also everyone dies in Adam's death.'[295] H. Vanlalauva says that the main emphasis of Zairema's theology of Original sin is trying to indicate that the sins of each and everyone has saturated the world and because of that everybody is responsible for transformation. In this case, no one is free from sin but everyone is responsible for the sin in this corrupted world.[296]

In Zairema's estimation the traditional view has an undesirable element of determinism in it, and does not sufficiently safeguard the responsibility of human. Like Liberal theologians, Zairema did not accept the teaching of original sin and Penal substitution theory of Atonement which is emphasized by Evangelical groups.[297] For

---

[291] The 'price' here, for Zairema, means that period during childhood when human beings desire maturity, even though he/she can do whatever he/she likes after maturity, they are much more bearing burdens. Zairema, *Genesis,* 25.

[292] Zairema, *Kan Bible Hi*, 261-262.

[293] Zairema, *Isua Rilru,* 231.

[294] Zairema, *Isua Rilru,* 231.

[295] Zairema, *Isua Rilru,* 231.

[296] Cited by Vanlalauva, "Rev. Dr. Zairema'n Chhandamna a Kalpui Dan, 20.

[297] In the teaching of Penal substitution theory, God cannot merely overtook human's sin, nor can God just forgive human without requiring that payment be

Liberal theologians, biological transmitted is impossible to accept. The normal meaning of substitution is to be taken in the context. It simply means that the atonement is a sacrifice offered in place of the sinner. Thus, the sacrifice bears the sinner's guilt.[298] Emil Brunner also does not accept the doctrine of Original sin in the traditional and ecclesiastical sense of the world. The first sin of the Adam was not and could not be placed to the account of all his descendants; nor did this sin result in a sinful state, which is passed on to his posterity, and which is now the fruitful root of all actual sin. He goes, "Sin is never a state, but it is always an act. Even being a sinner is not a state but an act, because it is being a person."[299] Bruner' estimation is closely related with Zairema's belief. Bruner says, "In Adam all have sinned – that is the Biblical statement; but how? The Bible does not tell us that. The doctrine of Original sin is read into it."[300] Indeed, according to Zairema, even though the biblical texts basing on Substitution theory are possible translated as 'substitute' or 'in behalf' from the root meaning (Gk. *huper*) but most of the English Bible translated *huper* as 'for.' If we translate it as 'substitute' or 'in behalf' there can be wrong conception for understanding the salvific work of Jesus. This theory lucidly declines human responsibility and duty and Jesus bears all the sins of human beings. It rejects the unity of God the Father and the Son.[301] When we critically study Zairema's understanding of Original sin and atonement from the passages of the Bible, it seems that it is acceptable and quite practicable because as H. Vanlalauva commended him he never tries to hide sin like Pelagius and Liberal theologians, he opined that over emphasizing Adam's sin rather than pretending not to know self - shortcoming

---

made or punishment be given for sin. In this sense, the atonement is necessary for human to be made right with his/her Creator.

[298] The Biblical passages for the Penal Substitution Theory of the Atonement are John 1:29; 2 Cor 5:21; Gal 3:13. House, *Charts of Christian,* 107.

[299] Louis Berkhof, *Introduction to Systematic Theology* (Grand Rapids, Michigan: Baker Book House, 1979), 249. (Hereafter will be cited as Berkhof, *Introduction to Systematic Theology,*).

[300] Emil Brunner, *Man in Revolt* (New York, 1939), 142. Cited by Berkhof, *Introduction to Systematic Theology,* 241.

[301] Zairema, *Kan Bible HI,* 285.

is not the teaching of the Bible. Realizing self-deficiency is a very biblical teaching.[302]

5) Faith: Zairema defined faith to mean depending upon God[303] and obedience to God.[304] Impossibility of existence without God is the meaning of our faith. His definition clearly indicated that faith is being depended upon the grace of God and faith is meaningless without grace.[305] Zairema opined that it is necessary to be careful in saying that it is totally the gift of God. He thought that due to the emphasis of faith as solely the gift of God, there is wrong conception of defining faith and many radical groups appeared among the Mizo who are neglecting to grow to be like Jesus in their daily life and are emphasizing the idea 'we cannot believe God, God gives us the ability to believe.' In the beginning, God created human beings with free will and knowledge of good and evil. God as well as the Tempter did not disregard human free will. Even when the power of God faces the cross it never disrespects human free will and knowledge of good and evil but faith and free will always move together. Thus, the grace of God also works in such manner for free will and faith to be able to go together.[306] In the protestant theology, salvation and faith is undividable. Justification by faith which means the action of pronouncing sinners righteous[307] is the theological methodology of Protestant Churches.[308]

H. Vanlalauva comments on Zairema's theology of salvation as dependable and very biblical. But, it appears that some of his theologies of sin are not biblical enough, yet at the same time from his perspective and research, it is appropriate with the biblical messages.[309] Although, his theology of sin and faith is unique to the

---

[302] Vanlalauva, "Rev. Dr. Zairema'n Chhandamna a Kalpui Dan, 20.

[303] Zairema, *Kan Bible HI,* 294.

[304] Zairema, *Lehkhabu Te Pasarih*, 39.

[305] Vanlalauva, "Rev. Dr. Zairema'n Chhandamna a Kalpui Dan, 25.

[306] Zairema, *Kan Bible HI....,* 292, cited by H. Vanlalauva, "Rev. Dr. Zairema'n Chhandamna a Kalpui Dan..., 26-27.

[307] House, *Charts of Christian...*, 94.

[308] Vanlalauva, "Rev. Dr. Zairema'n Chhandamna a Kalpui Dan, 25.

[309] Vanlalauva, "Rev. Dr. Zairema'n Chhandamna a Kalpui Dan, 30.

traditional way of teachings and it may be quite hard to understand; his stance and the reason why he expressed as such is truly biblical. On the other hand, when we look at Calvin's biblical hermeneutics, the role of the Holy Spirit becomes very important,[310] but even though Zairema realized that salvation is the work of God the Father, the Son and the Holy Spirit, yet he seldom expressed the Holy Spirit in his theology of salvation. Despite the fact that he was very much familiar with the church's doctrine, his lack of mentioning more of the work of the Holy Spirit leaves a big question.[311]

Transformation

As we already mentioned in the previous chapters, Zairema was also involved in many social transformations and in fighting corruption. When insurgency broke out in Mizoram, Zairema became one of the leaders of the Peace Mission and was arrested and imprisoned for 11 days[312] due to his role in the Peace Mission. Due to the efforts of the Peace Mission, a number of MNF leaders/volunteers were given amnesty by the government.[313] Since they were trying their best under Peace Mission to stop the suffering of the Mizo during insurgency period, Zairema and his co-workers Rev. Lalngurauva Ralte and Rev. H. S. Luaia were called the 'Three Blind Mice'[314] by A. Thanglura, the then Cabinet Minister of Assam.[315] He became Chairman of a voluntary social organization called Vigilance Committee which was changed to Mizoram Guardian from 1995. He submitted Public Interest Litigation (PIL) to the Supreme Court with his friend Bualhranga against the then Mizoram Chief Minister Lalthanhawla for corruption case during 1996-1999. Since he was an ordained minister, many people severely condemned him for

[310] H. Vanlalauva, *Doctrine of God: John Calvin's Doctrine of God With Special Reference to the Indian Context* (Delhi: ISCPK, 2006), 277. (Hereafter will be cited as Vanlalauva, *Doctrine of God,*).

[311] Vanlalauva, "Rev. Dr. Zairema'n Chhandamna a Kalpui Dan, 31.

[312] Zairema, *Isua Rilru*, 258.

[313] Zairema, *Isua Rilru,* 258-259.

[314] This is a derogatory term for them.

[315] Zairema, *Thukhawchang Mi Pekte Hi*, 139 & Zairema, *Isua Rilru,* 258-259.

his effort.[316] The activities of this voluntary organisation, includes among others, awareness drive of public responsibilities, discussing problems with all political parties and voluntary organisation, face to face discussion of corruption cases with concerned authorities. Because of his quest for peace and transformation of society he was mocked, condemned and criticised by many people but he never loses heart and become despondent. He remains firm in his conviction and what he understood of the Gospel of Jesus. In 1960, Zairema preached his famous sermon "He Cannot Save Himself" (Matt 27:42). It seems that his message influenced and strengthened his life for social transformation. He maintained that Jesus cannot save Himself but this resulted in the saving and healing of others from their body and psychological entrapment. He spoke:

> Today we talk of social service. But whoever hears of a man (sic) giving his all for others? It is just a common sense that what we can do for others we ought to do, but we should do the utmost for ourselves. But here, hanging on the cross, we have a foolish fellow, who used to save others, when the same thing happens to him he cannot do anything![317]

As Spindler comments Jesus' mission of Luke account, in Luke, proclamation in word is closely linked with concrete deeds of liberation breaking through the structures of oppression and injustice that force the poor into their situation of poverty and hold them there by violence. Mission thus aims to restructure society as a whole on a global scale.[318] Zairema's involvement on social transformation is quite appropriate with the teaching of Jesus.

Zairema theologised the cross and makes use it for social transformation. According to him, cross is the pointer of the love

---

[316] Bualhranga, "A Hniakhnung Zuiin," in *I Ni Min Pek Hi*..., 514. Thanseia, Discussion on "Zairema rilru (The Mind of Zairema)," in *Talk Show* on 3rd Dec. 2011, in Zonet Studio, Aizawl, organized by Rev. Zairema Memorial Society.

[317] Zairema, *Isua Rilru*, 45.

[318] M. R. Spindler, "The Biblical Grounding and Orientation of Mission," in *Missiology: An Ecumenical Introduction,* edited by F. J. Verstraelen, et al. (Grand Rapids, Michigan: William B. Eerdmans Publishing Company, 1995), 130.

of God. The full human being of Jesus suffered at the cross for humanity which was planned by God. God created human beings in God's likeness and for God's glory. But, the cross revealed the failing of fulfilment of our own destiny, the horribleness of sin and the imperfection of human beings. Although, the Pharisees and Sadducees crucified Jesus, our sin and their sin are similar. We crucified Jesus whenever we disobey God's instruction. Jesus' dying on the cross is not something which happened long ago, but it is the pointer to God's feeling which is hurt by human's sin even till today.[319] The hidden sin pains the heart of God, and the corporate sins cause world wars. He continues to say that if we want to help somebody, we need to go with him/her to the cross. There is no other place for reforming the nation and individual except through the cross. It is necessary to go with the nation to cross.[320] In the light of Zairema's theology of the cross, we can say that our God is a *Transforming God*, transforming the life of both individual and collective which is the will of God. Crucifying our old life to cross and renewing in likeness of God become the main purpose of the cross. When we look at Zairema's theology of the cross, it is very practicable for today Christian because the main aim of his theology of the cross points out that whatever our shortcomings and failure they crucified Jesus continually.

Social Gospel

As we have already pointed out in the previous chapter that the main message of social Gospel theology is collective salvation rather than individual salvation and realized eschatology - the Reign of God here on earth. Zairema was also very much influenced by this theology. But at the same time, he goes a step further than other social Gospel theologians. He thought that here and now is not sufficient but to continue in the life after death in Heaven.[321] When he preached the suffering of Jesus, he emphasized that Jesus' suffering causes healing, salvation and good relationship among human. He says, "When he

---

[319] Zairema, *Kan Bible HI,* 302.

[320] Zairema, *Kan Bible HI,* 303.

[321] Zairema, *Kan Bible HI,* 281.

met Jesus, Zacchaeus was completely changed and reformed. Jesus said, 'Today salvation has come to this house.' Salvation here means a right relationship with Jesus and so with God, and that is outwardly visible in character and dealing with others. His new relationship with Jesus made it possible for him to start life afresh and be something for God. Salvation begins here and now and is fulfilled in the life beyond."[322] While Social Gospel theology influenced Zairema, some of his fellow Mizo pastors cannot adopt this theology. Thansiama says that if we take up social Gospel theology, then there is no need of the Bible.[323] Lalsawma also says that 'Social Gospel Theology' cannot be acceptable but there can only be social concern theology.[324] It seems that Evangelical theology which is emphasizing soul saving ministry influenced his fellow pastors. When we look at Social Gospel theology, it is almost similar with Transformation theology. Every social transformation theology emphasized reducing of social evil practices and rebuilding the Kingdom of God here and now, and to perform liberation of any oppression. Meanwhile a criticism for this theology is that if we stress social transformation as a spiritual obligation, it cannot be relevant enough to our spiritual pilgrimage. It should be balanced with spiritual portion.

Conclusion

Zairema's theology therefore, bears the imprint of all the factors which were characteristic of the era in which he lived. Although, Zairema followed liberal approach in his biblical hermeneutics, he has uniqueness from other liberal theologians; he does not pursue all the theological implications of liberalism.[325] He was very biblical in his theological articulation. It is, therefore, true to say that Zairema's

---

[322] Zairema, *Isua Rilru*, 46.

[323] Interview with Rev. Thansiama, former Moderator of Mizoram Synod, Chhinga Veng, Aizawl, 17 December 2011.

[324] Interview with Rev. Dr. Lalsawma, former moderator and Sr. Executive Secretary, Mizoram Synod and a co-worker of Zairema in the Peace Mission, Mission Veng Thlang, Aizawl, 16 December 2011.

[325] Liberal theology implies: 1) Emphasizing rational and personal experience, 2) All religious belief will be appropriate with human reason and science, 3) No need to neither believe infallible nor give authoritative to the Bible, 4) No need

theology is not outdated and context-related. When we look at Zairema's biblical approach and his theological articulation we can know that he draws his materials from the Bible. But, it must be pointed out that Zairema is not a fundamentalist in his approach to the Bible. Lalsawma puts Zairema as a scientist-humanist pastor,[326] we can know from his Biblical approach Zairema gives humanity and good relationship among human beings as a pivotal role in his theology. We can conclude his theological stance as 'You shall love your neighbour as yourself' (Matt 19:19; 22:39; Mark 12:31).

to differentiate natural and super natural in every aspect, 5) Christianity will be clapped together with modern world. Zirsangliana, *Theology Kalphung,* 96.

[326] Interview with Rev. Dr. Lalsawma, systematic theologian, former moderator and Sr. Executive secretary, Mizoram Synod and a co-worker of Zairema in the Peace Mission, Mission Veng Thlang, Aizawl, 16 December 2011.

Chapter 5

Final Conclusion

In the light of our analysis and appraisal, it is evident that there are many factors which influenced Zairema's theology. At the same time, we cannot deny that Zairema's biblical approach has a number of weaknesses and limitations. Like other Christian theologies, it is a human construction in a particular historical context. Its nature, characteristics and functions all are conditioned by its own context. The British annexation and the advent of Christianity had profound effect on Mizo socio-economic, political and religio-cultural life. They were also led by an institutionalized Church which plays great role in shaping the moral and ethical values of the people. All of the historical contexts played an important role in shaping Zairema's theology.

Besides these, his theology was shaped by the church and political upheavals in Mizoram. He said that he could comprehend the solitude of Jesus at the cross as Zairema himself faced crisis in his life. He was arrested and imprisoned by the order of B. P. Chalih, the then Chief Minister of Assam during insurgency period of Mizoram. When polices towed him on the street, he thought that the people considered him as one of the convicted people. It was from such a situation that he formed his famous theology of the cross.[327] It is fair to say that many of his theological implications broke out from his desperate experiences.

Since liberation theology motivated him in his theological articulations, Zairema was very much concerned with the role of "Biblical Theology" for social dimension and he was in favour to change the Mizo approach to the Bible that it should be praxis oriented and not merely spiritual in orientation. His approach to the Bible contributed to providing a theoretical framework for social and moral reformation among the Mizo. He found the Bible to be very useful for transforming society and he involved himself for reforming the political and social life driven by his understanding of the word of God and his understanding of what Jesus' salvation means to human beings. He used the Bible as his entire theological stance and made use of the message of the Bible for transforming the society and he participated in socio-political reformation. When we look at Zairema's biblical approach and his theological articulation, though he draws his materials from the Bible, yet he made use 'Historical Critical Method' and 'Textual Criticism' of the Bible for implementing his biblical hermeneutics. Zairema is not a fundamentalist in the mean time he cannot be regarded as liberal theologian in its full sense, because he was different from other liberal theologians. In the light of his theological implications Zairema can be called scientist-humanist, and anthropologist pastor, as we know from his Biblical approach that Zairema gives humanity supreme importance, also he thought very highly of good relationship among human beings in his theology.

Due to the hatred of corruption and other social evils, Zairema was also deeply involved in social services. One of the writers of his memoirs says that Zairema strongly hold on to his motto: 'service to man [sic] is service to God,' throughout his life.[328] Though he never said that he was a God-fearing man (born again Christian), yet he

---

[327] Zairema, *Isuan Rilru*, 258-259.

[328] Zairema, *I Ni Min Pek Hi,* 422.

often told his close friends that his primary loyalty was to his Lord-God. He kept that loyalty till the end of his days.[329]

Since his understanding of salvation embraces all aspects of human beings focusing on both the realized and unrealized aspects. It seems that he tried to put into practice his cherished salvation notion which addresses the day-to-day realities. In 1957 he wrote his second book, *"Bilat Lei Hnathawh Dan"* (The Work of Cement). Many people could not understand as he was a theological graduate and made a sarcastic comment which goes, "The book by our first BD graduate!" At that time, Government of Mizoram released work order for construction of wellspring in various villages of Mizoram. But some corrupted contractors, who were not expert in cement construction, cheated the villagers, and their construction works did not last. So, Zairema was profoundly hurt by that case and wrote the book for the benefit of the people. Chuauthuama comments that, 'the book shows the immensity of Zairema's understanding of salvation.'[330]

In the light of the selected reading paradigms, it is visible that Zairema was highly interested in the concept of Reign of God here and now or realized eschatology which was inaugurated with the coming of Jesus and his ministry. As has been discussed throughout the study, it can be seen that realized eschatology is the chief cornerstone in Zairema's theology and in formulating his theology he was deeply influenced by his life experiences. He emphasized that Jesus' salvation includes every sphere of humankind. This is evident from what has been brought out in the fourth chapter of the study. The significance of realized eschatology, Reign of God here on earth lucidly fashioned Zairema's theology. In realized eschatology, Jesus changed the wrong conceptions of others and made a new covenant between God and human beings. The main aim of Christ's mission is to change the defected life of human beings, and to make reconciliation between

---

[329] Zairema, *I Ni Min Pek Hi,* 423.

[330] Chuauthuama, an ordained minister of Mizoram Synod and a Mizo Old Testament Scholar, says in Discussion on Seminar of "Rev. Dr. Zairema'n Chhandamna a Kalpui Dan (Zairema Theology of Salvation)" presented by H. Vanlalauva, organized by *Rev. Zairema Memorial Lecture Vawi Khatna* on 4th Mar. 2011.

God and human beings and also among human beings. In the realm of God's reign, peace, harmony and showing favour to one another, the mission of Jesus are bound by love, care, mercy and peace.

In the light of the appraisal, Zairema's theological implications prove to be very dependable from the perspective of systematic theology.[331] According to Paul Tillich, theology must serve the needs of the church. A theological system is supposed to satisfy two basic needs; the statement of the truth of the Christian message and the interpretation of this truth for every new generation.[332] Zairema tried to provide his biblical hermeneutics as relevantly as possible to the people. Tillich argued that systematic theology is not a historical discipline, it is a constructive task. It does not tell us what people have thought the Christian message to be in the past which is relevant to the present situation.[333]

Paul Tillich's three main sources of Systematic Theology[334] and Zairema's theological methodology are closely connected. Like Paul Tillich, Zairema accepts the fact that the Bible is the original or basic source of document on which the Christian church is founded. He rejected the Neo-Orthodox view that the Bible is the only source of systematic theology. He is of the opinion that biblical message could not have been received had there not been preparation for it in human history. Because the biblical message embraces more than

---

[331] Systematic theology, according to Lewis Sperry Chafer, is a science which follows a humanly devised scheme or order of doctrinal development and which purports to incorporate into its system all the truth about God and His universe from any and every sources It may be distinguished from Biblical theology, in that Biblical theology draws its material only from the Bible. It has been defined as the orderly arrangement of Christian doctrine; but as Christianity represents only a mere fraction of the whole field of truth relative to the person of God and God's universe, this definition is inadequate. Lewis Sperry Chafer, *Systematic Theology*, Vol. - I. (Grand Rapids: Kregel Publications, 1993), 5, 6.

[332] Paul Tillich, *Systematic Theology*, (Three volumes in one), 2nd Impression (Chicago: The University of Chicago Press, [1967], 1971), 3. (Hereafter will be cited as Paul Tillich, *Systematic Theology*,).

[333] Paul Tillich, *Systematic Theology*, 3.

[334] Paul Tillich's three main sources of Systematic Theology are 1) Bible 2) Church History 3) History of Religion and Culture.

the biblical books, systematic theology has other sources beyond the Bible.[335]

Tillich is of the view that church history cannot be avoided as it is both religiously as well as scholarly important. The relationship of systematic theology to the church tradition must not be ignored. A theologian can make use of all the materials provided by the church history that enables one to interpret the biblical message.[336] Zairema also make use of the history of the church for his theological implications and was concerned with the resolution of the church to be the voice of God. After he finished BD course Zairema sacrificed himself to the works of Mizoram Synod, he said, "When I offered myself to the Synod, I believe that where I will be listening to the voice of God is through the Synod, because of that I worked with contentment."[337] He said that in another place, "For the Roman Catholic church, the word of Pope is infallible and for the Mizoram Presbyterian Church the resolution of the Synod meeting is infallible. Firstly we should accept it, but if it is not relevant we will change in the next meeting.[338]

The impact that history of religion and culture has upon the systematic theologians begin with the language they use and the cultural education that they have received. A systematic theologians' spirituality is being shaped by the cultural elements of their immediate surroundings in all one's endeavours. Their existentiality becomes the means of one's attitude or expression, and the confirmation of their statement. The theology that was framed by all these elements seeks to answer the question that situation imposes.[339] As we mentioned before, Zairema wrote a *Religion of the Lushais (Mizo)* in his BD thesis, H. Vanlalauva believes that his research work pressed him to

---

[335] Paul Tillich, *Systematic Theology,* 35. Zairema also says that if there is no reliable norm for the rule of faith and conduct in Jesus' word and in the Bible itself, we base the tradition of the elders. If there is no tradition of the elders again, we use the voice of the assembly of the church and the words of God which are revealed in the mind of the Church members. Zairema, *Genesis,* viii.

[336] Paul Tillich, *Systematic Theology...,* 36-38.

[337] Zairema, *I Ni Min Pek Hi,* 221.

[338] Zairema, *Kan Bible Hi,* 239.

[339] Paul Tillich, *Systematic Theology,* 38.

appreciate the Mizo culture and primal religions. He made use of what he had discerned about the Mizo religion and culture in his Biblical interpretation and in the Bible translation work.[340]

Lalngurauva Ralte regarded him as 'versatile man'[341] rightly so because when we observe in the light of systematic theology, Zairema embraces church history, religion and culture beyond the Bible for his theological methodology. As we have seen, Zairema's theological methodology is, to a large extent, conditioned by his context. L. H. Rawsea, a Mizo NT Scholar made a remark about him by saying that the theology of Zairema will always have perennial relevance.[342] It must be noted that Zairema's theological methodology is not outdated and irrelevant. In our theological endeavour, Zairema's theological methodology can still provide us with help. In the light of Zairema's teachings, we can say that envisioning a new community through participation in the humdrum truth of life would bring about total transformation and liberation in all aspects of human existence.

---

340 H. Vanlalauva, "Rev. Dr. Zairema'n Chhandamna a Kalpui Dan, 5.

341 Rev. Dr. Lalngurauva Ralte, discussion on "Zairema rilru," in *Talk Show* on 3rd Dec. 2011, in Zonet Studio, Aizawl, organized by Rev. Zairema Memorial Society. And Interview with Rev. Dr. Lalngurauva Ralte, a close friend of Zairema and his co-worker in the Peace Mission, Mission Veng Thlang, Aizawl, 16 December 2011.

342 L. H. Rawsea, review of *Kan Bible Hi* by Rev. Dr. Zairema, *Didakhe* (September – October, 2003), 27.

Bibliography

Primary Sources

Zairema, Rev. *Chanchin Tha Johana Ziak Hrilhfiahna.* Aizawl: Synod Publication Board, 1974.

____________. *Chanchin Tha Marka Ziak Hrilhfiahna.* Aizawl: Synod Publication Board, 1970.

____________. *Genesis Bu Thlanchhuah Hrilhfiahna.* Mission Vengthlang: Jubilee K.T.P Branch. 1998.

____________. *I Ni Min Pêk Hi.* Aizawl: Zorun Community, 2009.

____________. *Isua Rilru.* Aizawl: Zorun: Community, 2009.

____________. *Kan Bible Hi.* Aizawl: The Author, 2003.

____________. *Lehkhabu Tê Pasarih.* Aizawl: Zorun: Community, 2009.

____________. *Pi Pute Biak Hi.* Aizawl: Zorun Community, 2009.

____________. *Random notes.* Aizawl: Zorun Community, 2009.

____________. *Thian lehkhathawn.* Aizawl: Zorun Community, 2009.

____________. *Thukhawchang mi pekte hi.* Aizawl: Zorun Community, 2009.

Books

Adam, A. K. M. *What is Postmodern Biblical Criticism?* Minneapolis: Fortress Press. 1995.

Aland, Kurt. & Barbara Aland. *The Text of the New Testament,* translated by Erroll F. Rhodes. Grand Rapids, Michigan: Wm B. Eerdmans Pub. Co. [1987], 1995.

Ariarajha, S. Wesley. *Gospel and Culture: An Ongoing Discussion Within the Ecumenical Movement.* Geneva: WCC, 1995.

Barth, Karl. *Church Dogmatics* I/1. Edinburg: T&T Clark, 1936.

Berkhof, Louis. *A Summary of Christian Doctrine.* 1960, Reprint. Edinburgh: The Banner of the Truth Trust, 2002.

Berkhof, Louis. *Introduction to Systematic Theology.* 1962, Reprint. Grand Rapids, Michigan: Baker Book House, 1979.

Black, David Alan. *New Testament Textual Criticism: A Concise Guide.* Grand Rapids, Michigan: Baker Academic, 1994.

Bosch, David J. *Transforming Mission: The Paradigm Shifts in Theology of Mission.* Maryknoll New York: Orbis Books, 1991.

Braaten, Carl. *History and Hermeneutics.* Philadelphia: Fortress Press, 1966.

Bray, Gerald. *Biblical Interpretation: Past and Present.* England: APOLLOS, 1996.

Brown, Colin. *Karl Barth and the Christian Message.* London: Tyndale Press, 1977.

Carr, Dhyanchand. *Sword of the Spirit: An Activist's Understanding of the Bible.* Geneva: WCC Publications, 1992.

Chafer, Lewis Sperry. *Systematic Theology.* Vol. – I &2. Grand Rapids: Kregel Publications, 1993.

Chaltuahkhuma. *Political History of Mizoram.* Second Edition. Aizawl: Vanthangi, w/o Chaltuahkhuma, 2001.

Chatterji, N. *Status of Women in the Earlier Mizo Society.* Aizawl: Tribal Research Institute, 1973.

Chuauthuama. *Kal Hmasate Hlutna.* Aizawl: The Author, 2009.

Cone, James H. *A Black Theology of Liberation.* Maryknoll, New York: Orbis Books, 1986.

____________. *Speaking The Truth: Ecumenism, Liberation, and Black Theology.* Grand Rapids, Michigan: William B. Eermans Publishing Company, 1986.

____________. *God of the Oppressed.* New York: HarperCollin Publishers, 1975.

Daly, Mary. *Beyond God the Father: Toward a Philosophy of Women.'* Boston: Beacon Press, 1973.

Gnanakan, Ken. *Kingdom Concerns A Theology of Mission Today.* Leicester: InterVarsity Press, 1989.

Government of Mizoram. Directorate of Art & Culture. *Mizoram District Gazetteers.* Aizawl. 1989.

Grenz, Stanley J. & Roger E. Olson. *20th Century Theology: God & the World in a Transitional Age.* Secunderabad: OM Books, 2004.

Gutierrez, Gustavo. *A Theology of Liberation*: *History, Politics and Salvation.* Translated and edited by Sister Caridad Inda and John Eagleson, 3rd Edition. Maryknoll, New York: Orbis Books, [1973], 1988.

House, H. Wayne. *Charts of Christian Theology and Doctrine.* Grand Rapids, Michigan: Zondervan Publishing House, 1992.

Jenkinson, William & Helene O'Sullivan. *Trends in Mission: Toward the Third Millennium.* Maryknoll, New York: Orbis Books, 1993.

Jones, Gareth. ed., *The Blackwell Companion to Modern Theology.* Oxford: Blackwell Publishing Ltd., 2007.

Kipgen, Mangkhosat. *Christianity and Mizo Culture: The Encounter Between Christianity and Zo Culture in Mizoram.* Aizawl: Mizo Theological Conference, 1997.

Ladd, George Eldon. *A Theology of the New Testament.* Revised Ed. Grand Rapids, Michigan: William B. Eerdmans Publishing Company, [1947], 1993.

Laldailova, J. F. *Bible Thlirna.* Aizawl: R. Lalrawna, 2003.

Lalnithanga, P. *Mizorama Politics Inlumleh Chhoh Dan.* Aizawl: The Author, 2008.

Lalrinawma, V. S. *Mizo Ethos: Changes and Challenges.* Aizawl: Mizoram Publication Board, 2005.

Lalsawma. *Kristian Thurin Zirna (A Study of Christian Theology).* Aizawl: SL & PB, 1998.

Lalthangliana, B. *Culture and Folklore of Mizoram.* New Delhi: Publications Division of Ministry of Information and Broadcasting, Government of India, 2005.

______________. *Rev. Dr. Zairema Leh Capt. C. Khuma Hnuhma.* Chhinga Veng: R.T.M. Press. 2005.

______________. *India, Burma & Bangladesh-a Mizo Chanchin.* Aizawl: Remkungi, 2001.

Lerner, Gerda. *The Creation of Patriarchy.* New York: Oxford University Press, 1986.

Lianhmingthanga. *Material Culture of The Mizo.* Aizawl: Tribal Research Institute, 1988.

Lightfoot, Neil. R. *How We Got The Bible*. Secunderabad, Andhra Pradesh: OM Books, 2005.

Lindbeck, George A. *The Nature of Doctrine: Religion and Theology in a Postliberal Age.* London: SPCK, 1984.

Lloyd, J. Meirion. *History of the Church in Mizoram.* Aizawl: Synod Publication Board, 1991.

Manual of Worship of the Presbyterian Church of India. Shillong: The Presbyterian Church of India, 2002.

McCall, A. G. *Lushai Chrysalis.* Aizawl: Firma KLM Private Ltd. 1977.

Metzer, Bruce M. *The New Testament, Its Background, Growth, and Content.* London: Abingdon Press, 1969.

Metzger, Bruce M. *The Text of the New Testament: Its Transmission, Corruption and Restoration.* Oxford: Clarendon Press, 1964.

Moltmann, Jurgen. *The Church in the Power of Spirit.* London: SCM Press, 1977.

Nirmal, Arvind P. *Heuristic Explorations.* Madras: The Christian Literature Society, 1991.

Nunthara, C. *Mizoram: Society and Polity.* New Delhi: Indus Publishing Company, 1996.

Pathil, Kuncheria & Dominic Veliath. Eds. *An Introduction To Theology.* Bangalore: Theological Publications of India, 2005.

Ralte, Vanlalnghaka. *Bible Hrilhfiahna (Biblical Hermeneutics).* Aizawl: Presbyterian Bible School, 2011.

Rauschenbusch, Walter. *A Theology for the Social Gospel.* New York: Abingdon Press, 1917.

Remthanga, H. *Mizoram Presbyterian Kohhran Synod Thurel Lak Khawm.* Vol.-II. (1951-1970). Aizawl: Synod Literature & Publication Board, 1998.

Ro, Bong Rin & Ruth Eshenaur, eds. *The Bible and Theology in Asian Contexts: An Evangelical Perspective on Asian Theology.* Bangalore: Asian Theological Association & The Association of Evangelical Theological Education in India. 1984.

Sangkima. *Mizos: Society and Social Change.* Guwahati: Spectrum Publications, 1992.

Sangkima. *Essays on The History of The* Mizos. Guwahati: Spectrum Publications, 2004.

Shakespeare, J. *The Lushei Kuki Clans, Part–I.* Aizawl: Tribal Research Institute, 1975.

Siama, V. L. *Mizo History.* Aizawl: Lengchhawn Press, 1953.

Singh, S. N. *Mizoram: Historical, Geographical, Social, Economic, Political and Administrative.* New Delhi: Mittal Publications, 1994.

Smith L. David. *A Handbook of Contemporary Theology: Tracing Trends & Discerning Directions in Today's Theological Landscape.* Grand Rapids, Michigan: Baker Book House, 1992.

Soulen, Richard N. *Handbook of Biblical Criticism.* Atlanta: John Knox: Press, 1976.

Stott, John. *Understanding the Bible.* 1972, Reprint. Bombay: Gospel Literature Service, 1984.

Sugirtharajah, R. S. ed. *The Bible and The Third World: Pre-colonial, Colonial and Postcolonial Encounter.* Cambridge: Cambridge University Press, 2001.

Sumithra, Sunand. *Christian Theologies From an Indian Perspective.* Bangalore: Theological Book Trust, 1995.

Tate. W. Randolph. *Biblical Interpretation: An Integrated Approach,* 3rd Edition. Peabody, Massachusetts: Hendrickson Publishers, Inc., [1991, 1997], 2008.

Thanzauva, K. *Theology of Community.* Aizawl: Mizo Theological Conference, 1997.

___________ ed. *Towards a Tribal Theology The Mizo Perspective.* Aizawl: Mizo Theological Conference, 1989.

Thanzawna, R. L. and C. G. Verghese. *A History of the Mizos.* Vol.-II. New Delhi: Vikas Publishing House Pvt. Ltd., 1997.

Thiselton, Antony C. *Hermeneutics: An Introduction.* Grand Rapids, Michigan: William B. Eerdmans Publishing Company, 2009.

__________________. *New Horizons in Hermeneutics: The Theory and Practice of Transforming Biblical Reading.* Grand Rapids, Michigan: Zondervan Publishing House. 1992.

Thomas, Norman E. *Classic Texts in Mission & World Christianity.* Maryknoll, New York: Orbis Books, 1995.

Tillich, Paul. *Systematic Theology.* (Three volumes in one). 2nd Impression. Chicago: The University of Chicago Press, [1967], 1971.

Tochhawng, Rosiamliana. *A Study of Ten Articles of Faith of the Presbyterian Church of India.* Delhi: ISPCK, 2007.

Vanlalauva, H. *Doctrine of God: John Calvin's Doctrine of God With Special Reference to the Indian Context.* Delhi: ISCPK, 2006.

Virkler, Henry A. *Hermeneutics: Principles and Processes of Biblical Interpretation.* Secunderabad: O.M Books, 1981.

Watson, Natalie K. *Feminist Theology.* Grand Rapids, Michigan: William B. Eerdmans Publishing Company, 2003.

Young, Norman J. *History and Existential Theology: The Role of History in the Thought of Rudolf Bultmann.* Philadelphia: The Westminster Press, 1969.

Zaithanga, V. L. *From Head-Hunting to Soul-Hunting.* Aizawl: Synod Printing Press, 1981.

Zirsangliana, B. *Theology Kalphung Hrang Hrangte.* Aizawl: Lalremsiami, 2011.

Zofa, Lalhmachhuana. *Mizoram General Knowledge.* 7th Edition. Aizawl: Lalhmachhuana Zofa, [2005], 2011.

Dictionaries and Lexicons

Steinberg, N. "Social Scientific Criticism." *Dictionary of Biblical Interpretation, k – z.* Edited by John H. Hayes, et al. Nashville: Abingdon Press, 1999, 478.

A Greek-English Lexicon of the New Testament. Translated and enlarged by J. M. Thayer. New York: American Book Company, 1889.

Botterweck, G. Johannes & Helmer Ringgren eds. *Theological Dictionary of the Old Testament.* Translated by John T. Willis. 1975, Reprint. Grand Rapids, Michigan: William B. Eerdmans Publishing Company, 1983.

Chhuanliana, R. *Grik – Mizo Lexicon (Layman's Guide to the New Testament Greek Grammar and Lexicon).* Aizawl: Lengchhawn Press, 2007.

Colwell, J. E. "Sin." *New Dictionary of Theology.* Edited by Sinclair B. Ferguson, et al., 1988, Reprint. Leicester, England: InterVarsity Press. 2005, 641-643.

Duffy, Stephen J. "Sin." *The New Dictionary of Catholic Spirituality.* Edited by Michael Downey. Bangalore: Theological Publication in India, 2003, 889-901.

Gamble, Harry Y. "Canon." *Anchor Bible Dictionary.* Vol – I, (A-C). Edited by David Noel Freedman. New York: Doubleday, 1992, 837-861.

Lorain, J. H. *Dictionary of the Lushai Language.* Calcutta: Royal Asiatic Society of Bengal, 1940.

Marshall, I. H. "Redemption." *New Dictionary of Theology.* Edited by Sinclair B. Ferguson, et al., 1988, Reprint. Leicester, England: InterVarsity Press, 2005, 560.

McKenzie, John L. *Dictionary of the Bible.* Bangalore: Asian Trading Corporation, 2002.

McRay, John R. "Canon." *The Dictionary of Bible and Religion.* Edited by William H. Gentz. Nashville, Tennessee: Abingdon Press, 1986, 177-179.

Ngurchhawna, R. K. Z. T. Sangkhuma, Lalzuia Colney. *Zotawng Dictionary.* Aizawl: The Authors, 1997.

Noll, M. A. "Social Gospel." *New Dictionary of Theology.* Edited by Sinclair B. Ferguson, et al., 1988, Reprint. Leicester, England: InterVarsity Press, 2005, 646-647.

The Oxford English Dictionary. 2nd Edition. Vol. XVIII. Oxford: Clarendon Press, 1989.

Trompf, Garry W. "Utopia." *The Encyclopedia of Religion Volume 15 Trad – Zwin.* Edited by Mircea Eliade et al. New York: Macmillan Publishing Company, 1987, 159-162.

Unger, Merill F. "Canon of Scripture." *Unger's Bible Dictionary.* Edited by Merill F. Unger. 3rd Edition. Chicago: Moody Press, [1957], 1975, 174-178.

Articles

Chrispal, Ashish. "Contextualization." In *Doing Mission in Context.* Edited by Sunand Sumithra & F. Hrangkhuma. Bangalore: Theological Book Trust, 1995, 1-15.

Hluna, J. V. "Mizo Society and Economy." In *Mizo Hnamzia leh Khawtlang Nun Siamthat.* Aizawl: Synod Publication Board, 1988, 92-118.

Lalchhuanliana, "Chanchintha Dak Harhna (the Revival Movement of Gospel Mail)," in *Harhna: Mizoram Revival Centenary Souvenir (1906-2006).* Edited by R. L. Thanmawia et al. Aizawl: Synod Revival Committee, 2006, 489-503.

Lasetso, Razouselie, "The Word of God and the Tribal Response." In *Dalit-Tribal Theological Interface: Current Trends in Subaltern Theologies.* Edited by James Massey & Shimreigam Shimray. ETC Jorhat & New Delhi: TSC/WSC & CDS, 2007, 171-194.

Lianzuala, P. L. "Towards A Theology of Mizo Tlawmngaihna." In *Towards A Tribal Theology The Mizo Perspective.* Edited by K. Thanzauva. Mizoram: Mizo Theological Conference, 1989. 54-62.

Mawrie, Barnes L. "Experience of the Tribal Historical, Political, Socio-Cultural Contexts: Quest for a Tribal Theology." In *Dalit-Tribal Theological Interface: Current Trends in Subaltern Theologies.* Edited by James Massey & Shimreingam Shimray. Jorhat & New Delhi: TSC/WSC & CDS, 2007, 82-100.

Manohar, Moses P. "Kingdom of God the Test of the Church." In *Church Towards Understanding Mission and Witness.* Edited by Moses P. Manohar. Chennai: ICSA/ISPCK, 2002, 20-35.

Mulholland Jr., M. Robert. "Sociological Criticism." In *New Testament Criticism and Interpretation.* Edited by David Alan Black and David S. Dockery. Grand Rapids, Michigan: Zondervan Publishing House, 1991, 297-316.

Nicholls, Bruce J. and Charles H. Kraft, "Anglo-America." In *Contextualization: Meanings, Methods, and Model.* Edited by David J. Hesselgrave and Edward Rommen. Grand Rapids, Michigan: Baker Book House, 1989, 48-69.

Ralte, Rodinmawia. "Mizo Pi Pute Thlarau Khawthlir Hmanga Mizo Kristian Siam That." In *Zoram Thar A Awm Thei Ang Em?* Edited by L. H. Rawsea, et al. Bangalore: Bangalore Mizo Association, 2011, 169-194.

Spindler, M. R. "The Biblical Grounding and Orientation of Mission." In *Missiology: An Ecumenical Introduction: Texts and*

Context of Global Christianity. Edited by F. J. Verstraelen, et al. Michigan: William B. Eerdmans Publishing Company, 1995, 123-142.

Thangchungnunga. "Mizoram Sumdawnna: Tun Hma leh Tun Hnu." In *Kristiante Rahbi Thar.* Edited by Lalchhuanliana. Aizawl: Synod Social Front Committee, 1991, 42- 46.

Thanzauva, K. "Theological Education for Social Transformation: A Feminist Perspective." In *Transforming Theology for Empowering Women: A Theological Hermeneutical Reflection In The Context of North East India.* Edited by R. L. Hnuni. Jorhat: ETC, Women Studies, 1999, 88-94.

Thomas, M. M. "The secular Ideologies of India and the Secular Meaning of Christ." In *Readings in Indian Christian Theology -1.* Edited by R. S. Sugirtharajah & Cecil Hargreaves. Delhi: ISPCK, 1993, 93-101.

Tochhawng, Rosiamliana. "Methodological Reflection on Theologizing Tribal Heritage in North East India." In *Theologizing Tribal Heritage: A Critical Re-Look.* Edited by Hrangthan Chhungi. Delhi: CWM, ISET-ECC, PCI, ISPCK, 2008, 19-29.

Vanlalauva, H. "Thurin leh Zirtirna Lama Mizo Kristiate Harsatna." In *Kum 100 Kristian Zofate Hmabak.* Edited by R. L. Rinawma, et al. Bangalore: Bangalore Mizo Christian Fellowship, 1994, 1-21.

Vashum, Ahao. "Emerging Vision of Indigenous/Tribal Theology." In *Dalit-Tribal Theological Interface: Current Trends in Subaltern Theologies.* Edited by James Massey & Shimreingam Shimray. Jorhat & New Delhi: TSC/WSC & CDS, 2007, 16-55.

Whiteman, Darrell L. "Contextualization: The Theory, the Gap, the Challenge." In *New Directions in Mission & Evangelization 3: Faith and Culture.* Edited by James A. Scherer & Stephen B. Bevans. Maryknoll, New York: Orbis Books, 1999, 42-53.

Zairema, "A Quest for Indigenous Expression of Christianity in Mizoram." In *Ground Works for Tribal Theology in the Mizo Context.* Edited by Rosiamliana Tochhawng et al. Delhi: ISPCK, 2007, 119-127.

Zamawia, R. "Peace and Development in Mizoram: A Political Dimension." In *Peace and Development in Mizoram Role of the State and Civil Society.* Edited by Jagadish K. Patnaik. Aizawl: Department of Political Science Mizoram University (A Central University), 2008, 72-83.

Journals

Azyu, Thasia T. "The System of Administration in South Mizoram With Special Reference to Chhomo Hlychho, Chief of Serkawr 1927-1956." *Historical Journal Mizoram* IV/1 (July, 2003): 13-21.

Harvey, Thomas. "Heresy Reconsidered: Why the Non-Western World is Rediscovering the Necessity of Theological and Ecclesial Definition." *Mizoram Theological Journal* XI &XII/3 (July–December, 2005): 25-41.

Hluna, J. V. "Political Development in Mizoram Since Independence." *Historical Journal Mizoram* VII/1 (December, 1997): 12-15.

Lalfakzuala. Book Review of *Kan Bible Hi* by Rev. Dr. Zairema. *Thu Leh Hla* (September, 2004): 32-40 & (October, 2004): 35-40.

Malsawmliana. "Khawnbawl Upa in Early Mizo Society." *Historical Journal Mizoram.* VII/1 (July, 2006): 41.

Ralte, Vanlalnghaka "A Brief History of Mizo Bible Translations." *Mizoram Journal of Theology* II/1 (January – June, 2011): 73-96.

Rawsea, L. H. Review of *Kan Bible Hi* by Rev. Dr. Zairema. *Didakhe* (September – October, 2003): 25-27.

Unpublished Documents

Chhangte, Zomuansanga. "Contribution of Zairema to the Church and Society in Mizoram." B. D. Thesis, Aizawl Theological College, 2005.

Chuauthuama. Discussion on Seminar of "Rev. Dr. Zairema'n Chhandamna a Kalpui Dan (Zairema's Theology of Salvation)." Paper presented by H. Vanlalauva. In *Rev. Zairema Memorial Lecture Vawi Khatna,* 4th March 2011.

Fai, Tha Lian. "The Significance of Karl Barth's Understanding of the Word of God for Contemporary Mizo Christianity." M.Th. Thesis, Senate of Serampore College (University), 1999.

Hranleh, V. L. Luaia. "An Ethical Appraisal of Economic Change in Mizoram 1972-1992." M.Th. Thesis, United Theological College, 1994.

Lallianzuala, R. "Kohhrana Rev. Zairema Sulhnu." In *2nd Rev. Zairema Memorial Lecture,* Unpublished Seminar Paper, 8th Mar 2012, 4-30.

Lalngaihthanga, C. "A Study of the Theological bases of the Mizoram Presbyterian Church Administrative System." M.Th. Thesis, Aizawl Theological College, 2009.

Lalnghakthuami. "A Theological Examination of the Selected Mizo Festivals (Chapchar kut, Mim Kut and Pawl Kut): Towards a Theology of Mizo Culture." M.Th. Thesis, United Theological College, 1995.

Lalnunzira, B. "Mizo Bible: A Study of Mizo Bible Translation." B. D. Thesis, Eastern Theological College, 1997.

Malsawmliana. "Megalithic Monuments of Mizoram: A Destructive Study." Ph.D Thesis, North Eastern Hills University, 2011.

Ralte, Rev. Dr. Lalngurauva. Discussion on "Zairema rilru (The Mind of Zairema)." In *Talk Show* on 3rd Dec. 2011, in Zonet Studio, Aizawl. Organized by Rev. Zairema Memorial Society.

Thanseia, Discussion on "Zairema Rilru (The mind of Zairema)." In *Talk Show* on 3rd Dec. 2011, in Zonet Studio, Aizawl. Organized by Rev. Zairema Memorial Society.

Vanlalauva, H. "Rev. Dr. Zairema'n Chhandamna a Kalpui Dan (Zairema's Theology of Salvation)." In *Rev. Zairema Memorial Lecture Vawi Khatna.* Unpublished Seminar Paper, 4th Mar. 2011.

Vardingliani. "Jesus' Concern for the Poor With Reference to Luke 6: 20-21 and Its Implications for the Ministry of Churches." B.D. Thesis, Senate of Serampore College, 1997.

Internet Source

"Age of Enlightenment." http://en.wikipedia.org/wiki/Age_of_Enlightenment, (3 March 2012).

"Biblical criticism." http://creationwiki.org/Biblical_criticism (1 Nov. 2011).

"Black Theology Liberation Ethics-Society." http://www.amazon.com/Black-Theology-Liberation-Ethics-Society/dp/0883446855/ref=cm_cr_pr_simst (15 Aug. 2010).

"Criticism of the Historical-Critical Method of Biblical Scholarship and its Place in Future Exegesis, Historical-Critical Method condemned by Pope St. Pius X – still operative?" http://veneremurcernui.wordpress.com/2012/02/21/historical-critical-method-condemend-by-pope-st-pius-x-still-operative/ (28 Feb. 2012).

"History of Mizoram." MIZRM\History of Mizoram.htm (1 Nov. 2011).

"Social Gospel." http://en.wikipedia.org/wiki/Social_Gospel (24 Nov. 2011).

"Waterbuffalo theology." http://sites.google.com/site/eggen4jc/water buffalotheology (17 Aug. 2011).

Personal Interview

Lalbiaktluanga, Rev. Former Moderator of Mizoram Synod. Bungkawn Tlang veng, Aizawl. Interview, 21 December 2011.

Lalsawma, Rev. Dr. Former Moderator and Sr. Executive Secretary, Mizoram Synod and a co-worker of Zairema in the Peace Mission, Mission Veng Thlang, Aizawl. Interview, 16 December 2011.

Luaia, Rev. Dr. H. S. One of the Bible Translation Members and a close friend and co-worker of Zairema, Ramzotlang, Lunglei. Interview, 20th April, 2011.

Ralte, Rev. Dr. Lalngurauva. Former Moderator of Mizoram Synod. A close friend and co-worker in the Peace Mission of Zairema, Mission Veng Thlang, Aizawl. Interview, 16 December 2011.

Rokhuma, Elder C. A close friend of Zairema, Mission Veng Thlang, Aizawl. Interview, 12 December 2011.

Thansiama, Rev. Former Moderator of Mizoram Synod. Chhinga Veng, Aizawl, Interview. 17 December 2011.

Newspaper

The Aizawl Post, June 30, 2011.

The Aizawl Post, December 17 & 18, 2010.

Vanglaini, July 20, 2011.